SIMPLE
FOOD
BIG
FLAVOR

Also by Aarón Sánchez

La Comida del Barrio

SIMPLE
FOOD
BIG
FLAVOR

Unforgettable Mexican-Inspired Dishes from My Kitchen to Yours

aarón sánchez
with jj goode

PHOTOGRAPHS BY **MICHAEL HARLAN TURKELL**

ATRIA BOOKS

New York   London   Toronto   Sydney   New Delhi

ATRIA BOOKS

A Division of Simon & Schuster, Inc.
1230 Avenue of the Americas
New York, NY 10020

First Atria Books hardcover edition November 2011

ATRIA BOOKS and colophon are trademarks of
Simon & Schuster, Inc.

For information about special discounts for bulk purchases,
please contact Simon & Schuster Special Sales at
1-866-506-1949 or business@simonandschuster.com.

The Simon & Schuster Speakers Bureau can bring authors
to your live event. For more information or to book an event,
contact the Simon & Schuster Speakers Bureau at
1-866-248-3049 or visit our website at www.simonspeakers.com.

Designed by Jason Snyder

Manufactured in the United States of America

1   2   3   4   5   6   7   8   9   10

Library of Congress Cataloging-in-Publication Data
Sánchez, Aarón.
Simple food, big flavor : Unforgettable Mexican-inspired dishes from my
kitchen to yours / Aarón Sánchez with J.J. Goode ; photographs by Michael
Harlan Turkell.
    p.   cm.
Includes index.
1. Cooking, Mexican. 2. Cookbooks. I. Goode, J.J. II. Title.
TX716.M4S258   2011
641.5972—dc22   2011007167

ISBN 978-1-4516-1150-2
ISBN 978-1-4516-1154-0 (ebook)

To my wife, Ife; my son, Yuma;
and my daughter, Sofia

CONTENTS

SIMPLE
FOOD
BIG
FLAVOR

INTROD

Some people's memories have a sound track, an Usher jam calling to mind a rowdy birthday or a Bon Jovi song bringing back an awesome first date—instead, my memories smell like *carnitas* frying in a pot and garlic roasting on a *comal*. That's what happens when your mom is Zarela Martinez, one of the best Mexican cooks there is.

I never forgot how powerful the flavors in the Mexican culinary arsenal are, the way just a few chipotles and a couple of garlic cloves could become something so good it could make you curse. And later in my life, the way a simple sauce could rocket my mind back to my mom's kitchen. When she'd cook for me and my friends in New York, setting a bright green pumpkin seed sauce or *sopes* crowned with some mouth-searing salsa in front of us, they'd ask, their eyes wide with excitement, "Aarón, what's that?" *That?* I'd think. *That's* love *right there.*

When I was a kid, I'd ask her to make *sopa seca,* a sort of Mexican-style pasta. She'd fry alphabets so they'd get all nutty, and simmer them with pureed roasted tomatoes and onions, cilantro, and a little chile. But she cooked more than just Mexican food. I remember these chicken wings with pineapple, soy, ginger, and scallions. Talk about delicious! I still can't make them quite like she does.

UCTION

Whenever we visited El Paso, the border town where I was born, I was reminded how she got so damn good at cooking. I'd get giddy before those trips, because it meant I'd get to have my grandma's beans, which are pretty much the greatest food on earth—well, aside from whatever else she made. When I got a little older, it dawned on me why it was all so delicious: she was never in a rush. Her beans would sit on the stove for what seemed like forever, getting tastier by the hour. Even after I'd learned to cook more complicated food, I never forgot how with patience and a little know-how, even the simplest dishes could be spectacular.

As a kid, I'd gaze into her pot as she stirred a deep brown mole or stare at poblanos blackening over the blue flame on the stovetop. When I got a little older, I started to chip in. At first, I was relegated to chopping vegetables. Maybe I got to put together an hors d'oeuvre. But I quickly graduated to toasting chiles, a simple but vital task. I caught on quickly—when you're from a family of cooks, like a family of athletes, you realize that there are some things you can just *do,* without necessarily being taught.

When I decided to work in kitchens, I wasn't after glory or fame. This was before the Age of the Celebrity Chef. All I knew was that I wanted to create the kind of joy that the women in my life created. But I knew I had to carve out my own path. So when I was still a teenager, I took off to New Orleans (where I swear I didn't see one Mexican) and started working for Paul Prudhomme, the chef who put the city on the national gastronomic map. I was thrilled by the food there, the delicious gumbo of Cajun, French, Italian, Creole, Native American, and Spanish influences that was as complex and satisfying as the best moles.

Paul became my mentor. He taught me how to season food properly. He taught me to think, really *think*, about what goes on in your mouth when you taste food. He taught me the difference between blackening and burning. What is it? About three seconds.

I went on to cook at Patria in New York for Douglas Rodriguez, another mentor who opened my eyes to ingredients and techniques that I'd never seen before. That's where I met and fell in love with aji amarillo, the delicious chile from Peru, and learned to make *sofrito,* the incredibly flavorful slow-cooked vegetables that make Cuban, Puerto Rican, and Dominican food so damn good.

The kitchen crew at Patria also taught me some life lessons. One night, I was doing my thing on the grill station. I was rocking it. Three hundred meals and zero complaints. I was pretty proud. I looked over at the sous-chef, Georgi, a guy I really respected, and said, "Hey, how come every time I mess up, you guys chew my butt like chum, but tonight I didn't even get one compliment?" He glared at me. "This isn't a popularity contest. When nobody says anything, that *is* a compliment."

By the time I finally ran my own kitchen, I had so much to draw from, so many different chefs and eating experiences that had shaped my culinary style. The result was cooking that broke down borders, that brought together ingredients and techniques that made so much sense but had been kept apart out of habit.

For this book, I decided to take all my incredible flavor memories and distill them into fifteen recipes, to cram all that flavor into magical sauces, purees, and pastes that you can keep in the fridge or freezer and pull out whenever you want to turn a simple collection of ingredients into a seriously tasty dinner. We're talking an easy but amazing spice rub, a practically effortless cilantro–pumpkin seed pesto, an easy homemade dulce de leche, and much more. Each chapter begins with one of these, and what follows is a bunch of great recipes that apply it. Take my Garlic-Chipotle Love, for example, a puree of four easy-to-find ingredients that'll become your secret weapon in the battle for good food. I zoom in on certain techniques and ingredients to make sure you're successful, then I tell you how to store it and show you how once you've made it, you're minutes away from mussels steamed with chipotle and beer; smoky, garlicky mashed potatoes; and hearty bean and butternut squash picadillo. I even show you all the ways it'll become a part of your everyday eating, whether you spread a little on your next burger or use it to spike your next salad dressing. I'm sure you'll come up with your own ideas as well. Then you'll have a "whoa" moment—those fifteen recipes are your ticket to nearly one hundred dishes.

Once you've got an arsenal like this, your food will go from inspiring smiles and polite nods to igniting ridiculous grins and bear hugs.

garlic-chipotle love

This is one of my favorite sauces on the planet, something I'd swim in if I could. And it's dead simple, too: you roast some garlic and blend it with canned chipotles in adobo (an incredibly delicious product available in major supermarkets, not just bodegas), cilantro, and a little lime zest. Then, *papi,* you've got a foolproof sauce that I call Garlic-Chipotle Love because it's a distillation of one of my favorite flavor memories. The mellow sweetness of slow-roasted garlic paired with the smoky, spicy punch of these chiles always takes me back to my mom's kitchen.

When my mom's doing the cooking, those two fantastic flavors come together in a more traditional way. I remember watching her patiently toast the chiles and roast the garlic on a flat pan known as a *comal,* wondering why anyone would spend time doing this instead of watching *Knight Rider.* But by the time she was done, the whole house would smell, well, like love. We'd sit down to a simple dinner of, say, beans and chicken, and whatever salsa she had made with those chiles and garlic would make every bite explode with this comforting, ridiculously delicious love.

My version is built on hers and distills the same powerful flavors and aromas—with about a quarter of the effort. You could spread this sauce like butter on bread if you want, and you'll be loving life. Even better, this easy condiment, which will keep in your fridge for weeks or in your freezer for up to a month, can become multiple dishes that everybody at your table will go crazy for, even if my mom shows up for dinner.

garlic-chipotle love

MAKES 1 CUP

1 cup canola oil

12 garlic cloves, peeled

3 tablespoons chopped canned chipotle
    chiles in adobo sauce

¼ cup chopped fresh cilantro

Grated zest of 1 lime

1 teaspoon salt

1. Preheat the oven to 300°F.

2. Pour the oil into a heavy ovenproof
medium saucepan and add the garlic. Cover
the pot with foil, put it in the oven, and cook
until the garlic turns a nutty brown and is
really soft (think cream cheese), about 45
minutes.

3. Remove the pot from the oven and let the
garlic and oil cool to room temperature.

4. Put the garlic and the now garlic-infused
oil in a food processor or blender. Add the
chipotles and sauce, cilantro, lime zest,
and salt and puree until the mixture is
very smooth.

5. Store in the fridge in a tightly covered
container for up to 2 weeks or freeze for up
to a month.

SIMPLE WAYS TO USE IT

- Give your next burger a smoky, spicy lift by spreading some on the bun, or mix it with mayo and spread that on your burger.

- A spoonful turns dull soup into eye-rollingly good stuff.

- Push those bottled salad dressings to the back of the fridge. All you need to make salad sing like Shakira is 1 tablespoon Garlic-Chipotle Love, ¼ cup olive oil, and 2 tablespoons freshly squeezed lime juice.

- Use it as a flavor-infusing marinade for chicken, pork, or any other protein that used to run, fly, or swim.

- For an off-the-hook whole roast chicken, blend ½ cup Garlic-Chipotle Love with ½ pound (2 sticks) butter, perhaps tossing in some sturdy, *pollo*-friendly fresh herbs like sage, thyme, or oregano. Let the chicken come to room temperature, then spread the Love butter generously under the skin. Roast the bird in a 375°F oven for about 1½ hours.

- Make chipotle mayonnaise: In a mixing bowl, whisk together 1 cup mayonnaise, 2 tablespoons Garlic-Chipotle Love, 1 tablespoon finely chopped fresh chives, and 2 teaspoons freshly squeezed lime juice until they're thoroughly mixed. Season with salt and pepper to taste, and chill it until you're ready to serve it.

GARLIC: COOK IT RIGHT

Admit it: Last time you cooked garlic, you tossed bits of it into scalding oil. You happily watched them dance around until all of a sudden they were burning (often even before the garlic was fully cooked) and you freaked out. The result was bitter nastiness. It's cool; I see that mistake made again and again, whether people are cooking garlic in a pan or the oven. You're not alone, and we will get through this. Here's what you need to know: Garlic is like a good woman—you don't ask her to spend the night right away; you have to take it slow. So start with a *cold* pan. Put in your oil and garlic, then put it on the burner. My recipe for Garlic-Chipotle Love applies this principle but takes it to another level. The cloves get immersed in oil, the pan gets covered in foil, and in they go to a low oven. After 45 minutes, you have these nut-brown cloves that are mellow, sweet, and as soft as cream cheese, plus lovely garlic-infused oil. (If you want to be fancy about it, you could call the result garlic confit.)

THE OIL

Of course I want you to make the entire sauce, but if you're feeling lazy or just love garlic, you can stop after you've roasted the cloves. You'll have soft, sweet garlic to spread on bread and all that garlicky oil left behind to play with. You can drizzle it over steaks, or really get jiggy and use it instead of plain old vegetable oil to make an amped-up fresh mayonnaise. You can even add spices to the oil (I love to throw in a few bay leaves, dried chiles de árbol, and fresh thyme) before simmering the garlic in it. Then once the garlic is done, you strain the oil, store the oil and garlic separately, and pat yourself on the back. Oh, and because the garlic is the main event, I use oil with a neutral flavor, such as canola. But feel free to substitute olive oil if that's all you have in the house.

CANNED CHIPOTLES IN ADOBO

You'll never catch me without a can of chipotles in adobo in my pantry. That's because it's one of the best weapons in my cooking arsenal—a machine gun of flavor, the dynamite of deliciousness. Chipotle chiles begin as fresh jalapeños, which are then smoked and dried until they look like giant reddish-purple raisins and taste so different that their name just had to change. There are a few different varieties of chipotles, including one called *chipotles mecos*, which are a light brown color and larger than *chipotles moras*. Either way, it's an unbelievably delicious chile that's typically toasted in a dry pan and used in salsas and other sauces. When they're canned, these yummy buggers lounge in a tangy tomato and spice spa, and the result is ready to eat—no toasting necessary. This is the best canned product on earth—a little sweet and tangy, a lot smoky, and just spicy enough to get your lips tingling. And the best part is that it's available in just about any supermarket from Boise to Boston.

LIME ZEST

Citrus skin is packed with aromatic oils, and I love to add it to sauces to give them an extra layer of awesomeness. The key when you zest is to make sure you're getting the fragrant skin and not the bitter white pith. Thanks to their ultrathin blades, Microplane graters are the best tool for the task. If you don't have one, zest away anyway, but do it carefully.

NO FOOD PROCESSOR? NO PROBLEM

The food processor effortlessly turns the ingredients of Garlic-Chipotle Love into a slightly chunky paste. But if you don't have one, don't sweat it! Put all the components except for the oil on a cutting board and start chopping them up with a nice, heavy knife. When it's all chopped pretty fine, use the flat side of the blade to mush and scrape it against the board. Keep alternating— chopping and mushing, chopping and mushing—until you have a pretty smooth, rust-colored paste. Then transfer it to a bowl and gradually add the oil, stirring like a madman as you do.

STORE IT

Sure, you can whip up Garlic-Chipotle Love when you're ready to make my Mussels with Beer (page 10) or Smoky Black Bean Sauce (page 16), but there's no reason to wait. I want you to have this lying around so that when you're ready to cook, you'll reach into your fridge past the ketchup and mustard and mayo to something even tastier. So make it now, because it'll keep in your refrigerator in a plastic storage container for up to two weeks or in a freezer bag for up to a month. Or freeze it in ice cube trays, and once it's frozen, put the cubes in freezer bags—that way, you can use a little bit at a time, straight from the freezer.

mussels with beer and garlic-chipotle love

Mussels and beer already make a killer combo. You can thank the Belgians for coming up with it. But just a tablespoon of my Garlic-Chipotle Love takes the partnership to a whole new level. The smokiness and heat go so well with the beer (don't you dare think brews aren't taken seriously south of the border) that you'll forget about the Belgians and start praising me and my fellow Mexican cooks!

SERVES 4 AS AN APPETIZER

1 tablespoon extra virgin olive oil

1 small red onion, thinly sliced

1 large tomato, seeded and thinly sliced

1 tablespoon Garlic-Chipotle Love (page 6)

2 cups Mexican dark beer

1 pound mussels, debearded and scrubbed

Salt

Toasted bread or warmed tortillas,
   for serving

Cilantro leaves, picked off their stems, for
   garnish

1. Heat the olive oil over medium heat in a large skillet with a lid. Add the onion and tomato and cook, stirring occasionally, until the onion is soft and translucent, about 8 minutes.

2. Stir in the Garlic-Chipotle Love and beer. Add the mussels, cover the skillet, and cook until the mussels open. Discard any that don't open after 10 minutes. Season with salt to taste.

3. Serve in shallow bowls with plenty of toasted bread or warm tortillas for dipping. Garnish with fresh cilantro leaves.

pomegranate and roasted pepper salsa for raw oysters

I f you really want to party with oysters, you have to know when to ditch the cocktail sauce. This salsa is so much more lively—a little tart, a touch sweet, with some smoky, spicy love. It takes almost no time to make. Then you pop open those bad boys, or have your fish store open them for you, and you're good to go. Big thanks to the cohost of my first Food Network show, Alex Garcia, for helping me dream this up!

MAKES ABOUT 2½ CUPS, ENOUGH FOR 3 DOZEN OYSTERS

3 pomegranates

6 medium red bell peppers

1 tablespoon Garlic-Chipotle Love (page 6)

1 medium red onion, very finely chopped

1 tablespoon finely chopped fresh mint leaves

2 tablespoons olive oil

Juice of 2 limes

Salt and freshly ground black pepper

1. Cut the pomegranates into quarters and remove the seeds. The easiest way to do this is to peel back the rind on each quarter, pulling off the inner membrane to let the seeds fall into a bowl. Reserve a small handful for garnish. Extract the juice from the rest of the pomegranate seeds by putting the seeds in a sieve over a bowl and pressing down with a large spoon. Discard the naked seeds.

2. Turn three of your stove's burners to medium-high. Place 2 bell peppers on each burner and roast them, turning them occasionally with tongs, until they're charred all over and soft but not mushy, about 7 minutes. Transfer them to a big bowl or soup pot, cover it tightly with plastic wrap, and let the peppers steam for 10 minutes.

3. Peel the peppers (do not rinse off the skins), cut out the stems, and get rid of the seeds and veins. Finely chop the roasted peppers and add them to the pomegranate juice.

4. Stir in the Garlic-Chipotle Love, onion, mint, olive oil, and lime juice. Season with salt and pepper to taste. Serve the sauce alongside oysters on the half shell. Garnish with the reserved seeds. The sauce can be stored tightly covered in the refrigerator for up to 4 days.

NOTE: If you don't have a gas stove, put your peppers on a baking sheet and cook them under the broiler until they char, turning several times, about 10 minutes all together.

bean and butternut squash picadillo

This hearty combo of vegetables, with a little bacon and my Garlic-Chipotle Love in there to rev up the flavor, is so easy to make. Serve it along with a little rice and maybe some salsa, and you've got yourself a kick-ass meal.

SERVES 6

¼ pound (4 or 5 slices) thick-cut bacon, chopped

1 medium white onion, finely chopped

1 large red bell pepper, stemmed, seeded, and coarsely chopped

2 garlic cloves, very finely chopped

2 quarts chicken stock (low-sodium store-bought is fine)

1 medium butternut squash (about ¾ pound), peeled, seeded, and cut into ½-inch cubes

One 28-ounce can or two 15-ounce cans black-eyed peas, drained and rinsed

2 tablespoons Garlic-Chipotle Love (page 6), or more to taste

1½ cups corn kernels, fresh or frozen

¼ cup thinly sliced fresh basil leaves

Salt and freshly ground black pepper

1. Cook the bacon in a medium stockpot or Dutch oven over medium heat until it's lightly browned and has rendered its fat, about 5 minutes. Add the onion, bell pepper, and garlic and cook until the onion is tender and translucent, about 6 minutes. Pour in the chicken stock and add the squash cubes. Bring to a boil, then reduce the heat and simmer, stirring occasionally, until the squash is tender, 15 to 20 minutes.

2. Add the black-eyed peas, Garlic-Chipotle Love, and corn. Simmer until the picadillo has thickened and the flavors come together, about 12 minutes.

3. Stir in the basil and salt and pepper to taste. Divide among six bowls, and serve with rice and salsa.

smoky black bean sauce

Hey, there's nothing wrong with serving beans in a bowl. But turning them into a smooth, smoky sauce makes for an easy, elegant change of pace. I love to serve it with Chiles Rellenos (page 47) or Grilled Pork Tenderloin (page 36), but the possibilities are endless.

MAKES ABOUT 3 CUPS

1 tablespoon extra virgin olive oil

½ cup chopped white onion

½ cup Garlic-Chipotle Love (page 6)

1 tablespoon dried whole oregano
  (preferably Mexican)

2 cups drained black beans (cooked yourself
  or rinsed canned)

Salt and freshly ground black pepper

1. Heat the olive oil in a medium saucepan over medium heat. Add the onion, Garlic-Chipotle Love, and oregano and cook, stirring occasionally, for 5 minutes.

2. Add the black beans and ½ cup water, stir well, and cook for another 5 minutes.

3. Puree the mixture in a blender until it's smooth. Season with salt and pepper to taste. Store leftovers tightly covered in the refrigerator for up to 2 weeks.

chipotle-garlic mashed potatoes

Nothing goes better with mashed potatoes than my Garlic-Chipotle Love. Okay, maybe butter, so I added that, too.

SERVES 6

1 whole head garlic

1 tablespoon extra virgin olive oil

Salt and freshly ground black pepper

6 large russet potatoes (about 2½ pounds)

1 cup whole milk

4 tablespoons (½ stick) unsalted butter

¼ cup Garlic-Chipotle Love (page 6)

1. Preheat the oven to 375°F. Cut about ¼ inch off the top of the head of garlic and place the head, cut side up, on the center of a square of foil. Drizzle it with the olive oil and sprinkle it with salt and pepper. Wrap the head tightly in the foil and roast in the oven until the garlic is tender and caramelized, 50 minutes to 1 hour. Remove from the oven, unwrap, and let cool to room temperature.

2. While the garlic is roasting, peel the potatoes and cut them into quarters. Put the potatoes into a large saucepan, cover them with cold water, and add 1 teaspoon salt. Bring to a boil, then reduce the heat and simmer until the potatoes are tender, about 15 minutes. Drain the potatoes and put them back in the saucepan.

3. Heat the milk and butter in the microwave or in a small saucepan until just hot, not boiling. Squeeze the softened garlic into the potatoes and use a potato masher or a hand mixer to mash the potatoes and garlic together, whipping in the milk and butter and the Garlic-Chipotle Love. Season to taste with salt and pepper. Serve at once.

NOTE: If you need to hold the potatoes, smooth the surface and pour a ¼-inch layer of hot milk over the top. Cover the saucepan and keep the potatoes warm on the back of the stove. Just before serving, beat in the additional milk.

salsa verde

Think about the first dude to use a wheel-shaped stone to help him transport his spears, woolly mammoth meat, or whatever people carried around way, way back in the day. After he figured that out, I bet you he never went back to hauling that stuff on his back. That's sort of how it was for me when I first tasted chimichurri sauce done really well—nothing was ever the same again. Next thing I knew, I was making grilled steak after grilled steak, wondering why I had ever considered putting anything else on top.

Chimichurri is an herb vinaigrette that Argentinean people get down with like Germans do with mustard, like Americans do with ketchup. It speaks to the remarkable simplicity of a lot of Latin food, a few ingredients (in this case, parsley, garlic, vinegar, and oil) coming together to give you a crazy amount of flavor.

But check it out, I'm Mexican, okay? I know a little something about crazy amounts of flavor. So I decided to add a little something to chimichurri to make it even better and turn it into salsa verde: fresh cilantro and jalapeño chiles. The fresh cilantro gives you a blast of its matchless flavor, and the chiles make the sauce just lip-tingling enough to get things interesting but not enough to knock you back. There's occasionally some dried chile in the traditional version, but to me, adding fresh chile is even tastier, its grassy flavor going so well with all those herbs. And when something's this good, there's no way I'm reserving it exclusively for steak saucing.

salsa verde

MAKES 2 CUPS

¼ cup distilled white vinegar

2 jalapeños or 1 serrano chile, roughly
    chopped (yup, seeds too, if you can
    take the heat)

4 whole garlic cloves, peeled

4 dried bay leaves, crumbled

½ cup chopped fresh flat-leaf parsley
    leaves

½ cup chopped fresh cilantro

¼ cup chopped fresh oregano

1 cup olive oil

Salt and freshly ground black pepper

1. Combine the vinegar, jalapeños, garlic, and bay leaves in the blender jar and puree until smooth. Strain through a fine-mesh sieve into a bowl. Stir in the herbs. Pour the olive oil in slowly and steadily, whisking the whole time. Season with salt and pepper to taste.

2. Store in the refrigerator in a sealed container and use within a week.

SIMPLE WAYS TO USE IT

- Just try to find meat or seafood that doesn't taste amazing drizzled with a little salsa verde. Scallops, salmon, chicken, steak, pork—they're all good, especially if they're fresh off the grill.

- You know those guys who think they don't like vegetables? Grill some peppers, zucchini, and onions, toss on some of this green potion, and they'll change their tune.

- Double up on flavor—marinate your meat or fish in salsa verde (fish tacos!), and hit it again with the sauce after you've cooked it.

- Be creative: Don't be afraid to throw in chopped roasted red peppers, sun-dried tomatoes, olives, or fresh tomatoes to make the sauce even more colorful and substantial.

- It makes a perfect match with meat, but it's really just a vinaigrette—so treat it like one and use it to dress your next salad.

MAKING IT HAPPEN

You'll notice that in the recipe, I ask you to blend the vinegar, garlic, and chiles but not the herbs. Hand chopping the herbs and then adding them to the sauce is the key to a perfect salsa verde that'll stay bright green and vibrant. Remember, it's a vinaigrette, not a puree.

STORING SALSA VERDE

Because it's so versatile, you'll always want some around. And you're in luck—you can keep the sauce in the fridge for up to a week. Just let it come to room temperature and give it a good stir before you serve it. To keep the color from fading too much, pour ¼ inch of olive oil over the surface before you put the lid on. It forms an airtight seal that helps keep it green.

HOT-BUTTON ISSUE

I love spiciness. It balances sweetness and saltiness, it adds another layer to food, and it's just plain exciting. But I grew up eating hot stuff. I know that not everyone feels the same love for it that I do. So whether you have a low tolerance or just don't like the heat, you're not out of luck. Here are your options: Use a knife to scrape out the seeds and veins from the chiles (that's where a lot of the heat lives), use one chile instead of two, or leave them out altogether. You'll still get a tasty result.

WASH AND DRY

Fresh herbs are so easy to use. All you have to do is wash them and dry them. Too bad so many people mess up that part. What you *don't* want to do is spray water on those delicate herbs or manhandle them with paper towels. Instead, fill a large bowl (or even better, a salad spinner) with cold water, add the herbs, gently swish them around, and let them sit for a bit. Any dirt or grit will settle to the bottom. Take them out of the water (submerge them again in fresh water if they're very dirty), and either spin them dry (my favorite way) or drain them well and gently pat them dry with paper towels. You can do this several days before you're ready to use them if you wrap them in a damp paper towel and store them in a sealed plastic bag.

tomato salad with queso fresco

When you find perfect summer tomatoes heavy with juice, you don't have to do much to make a nice salad. The sweet crunch of red onion, some crumbled salty cheese, and maybe some chile, sliced as thin as you can manage—that's about it. Yet a drizzle of my flavor-packed Salsa Verde turns it into a kick-ass salad, which, believe me, is much better than a nice one.

SERVES 2

2 large tomatoes, cored

1 small red onion, thinly sliced

1 serrano chile or 2 jalapeños, very thinly sliced (yup, seeds too, if you can take the heat)

1 tablespoon chopped fresh cilantro

½ cup crumbled queso fresco (preferably the Cacique brand) or lightly salty feta

2 tablespoons Salsa Verde (page 20)

Salt (preferably coarse, crunchy sea salt)

Freshly cracked black pepper

Cut the tomatoes into ¼-inch-thick slices and arrange them on a plate with the onion. Sprinkle the chile and cilantro on top and around the plate. Crumble the queso fresco on top. Drizzle on the Salsa Verde. Season with salt and pepper to taste and serve immediately.

roasted batata salad
with salsa verde

Sometimes I like to douse sweet potatoes in brown sugar and butter, but I also love to go the savory route, tossing simple roasted batatas, a lovely super-starchy tropical variety, with cumin and Salsa Verde, which adds an herbal punch, acidity, and spice. The only thing it's missing is the calories.

SERVES 4

4 medium batatas (about 2 pounds; see Notes)

1 teaspoon ground cumin

½ cup Salsa Verde (page 20), or more to taste

Salt and freshly ground black pepper

1. Move a rack to the middle of the oven and preheat the oven to 400°F.

2. Wrap each batata individually in a square of aluminum foil. Put the batatas on the oven rack, leaving space between them for the heat to circulate. Roast until the batatas feel tender when gently squeezed, about 1 hour. Depending on the size of your batatas, they may need as long as 90 minutes to become tender, but check them, squeezing lightly with an oven mitt, after 1 hour.

3. While the batatas are roasting, toast the cumin: Heat a dry cast-iron skillet or small heavy saucepan over medium-low heat. Add the cumin and stir for about 1 minute, just until it smells fragrant. Pour it into a small bowl (it will scorch if you leave it in the pan) and set it aside.

4. When the batatas are tender, remove them from the oven and let them cool in the foil for about 15 minutes, until they're cool enough to handle.

5. Unwrap the batatas and peel off the skins. Cut them into ½-inch cubes and put them in a serving bowl. Toss gently with the toasted cumin and Salsa Verde. If the batatas look dry, add another few tablespoons of the Salsa Verde. Season with salt and pepper to taste. Serve warm or at room temperature.

NOTES: Feel free to substitute regular sweet potatoes, or even combine batatas or sweet potatoes with russets. Be creative!

If you like, you can grill the batatas: Wrap in heavy-duty foil, place over indirect heat on an outdoor grill, and turn occasionally until tender, about 1 hour.

octopus and squid salad

Here's a fantastic seafood salad that's exciting enough to serve as a party appetizer but hearty enough for a main course along with some warm tortillas. It's got major flavor from olives and my Salsa Verde, plus I throw tasty hearts of palm in there for good measure. And I know what you're thinking, but you *can* cook octopus at home! In case you're not up for it, you can substitute shrimp barely poached in simmering water. Drain them, pat them dry, then grill them with the squid.

**SERVES 8 AS AN APPETIZER
OR 4 AS A MAIN**

One 5-pound octopus, thawed if frozen

2 dried bay leaves

4 lemons, 2 cut in half and 2 juiced

3 whole black peppercorns

½ cup dry white wine

Hot sauce

1 pound cleaned squid, with the tentacles cut into bite-size pieces

Olive oil

Salt

2 tomatoes, seeded and diced

1 medium red onion, finely chopped

4 scallions, thinly sliced

2 cups drained chickpeas (cooked yourself or rinsed canned)

¼ cup pitted kalamata olives, sliced

¼ cup Salsa Verde (page 20), or more to taste

5 annatto seeds

4 garlic cloves, thinly sliced

Two 14-ounce cans hearts of palm, drained and quartered lengthwise

Lemon wedges, for garnish

1. Combine the octopus, bay leaves, halved lemons, peppercorns, white wine, and a few dashes of hot sauce in a stockpot. Add 3 to 4 quarts water to cover. Cook, covered, over medium-low heat until the octopus is very tender, about 2 hours.

2. Let the octopus cool in the liquid until you can handle it, then remove it from the liquid. Peel off the outer layer. Cut the octopus into bite-size pieces.

3. Put the squid on a cutting board and cut them lengthwise so you can open them flat.

(continued)

4. Combine the squid and octopus in a large bowl. Drizzle on ¼ cup olive oil, season with salt, and toss well. Heat a grill pan or large cast-iron skillet over medium-high heat until hot but not smoking. Working in small batches to avoid crowding the pan, cook the squid and octopus just until the squid is cooked through, about 2 minutes. Transfer to a plate to cool to room temperature. Cut the squid into thin strips.

5. Combine the squid, octopus, tomatoes, onion, scallions, chickpeas, and olives in a clean large bowl. Add the Salsa Verde, toss well, season with salt and more Salsa Verde to taste, and set aside. (Even if you stop here, you're in for a treat.)

6. Heat ¼ cup olive oil and the annatto seeds in a medium skillet over medium heat until the oil is deep gold. Scoop out the seeds with a slotted spoon and discard them. Add the garlic and cook, stirring often, until it's golden brown. Add the hearts of palm and cook until they have browned, about 5 minutes. Add the lemon juice and season with salt to taste. Divide the hearts of palm among serving plates and distribute the salad on top. Serve right away, garnished with lemon wedges.

clams with salsa verde

Y ou'd better grab the crusty bread, because you're going to have a lot of sopping up to do. Once you suck down all those briny, meaty clams, you're left with the amazing soupy sauce that's extra bright with the herbs and acidity from my Salsa Verde.

SERVES 4 AS AN APPETIZER

1 tablespoon olive oil

4 garlic cloves, thinly sliced

1 pound Manila clams or cockles, scrubbed

½ cup dry white wine

1 cup bottled clam juice or fish stock (homemade or store-bought)

¼ cup Salsa Verde (page 20)

Salt and freshly ground black pepper

Grilled sliced crusty bread, for serving

1. Combine the olive oil and garlic in a large, deep skillet. Put the pan over medium heat and cook, stirring often, until the garlic is golden brown, about 5 minutes. Be careful not to burn the garlic.

2. Add the clams and cook for 2 minutes. Add the wine and clam juice, shake the pan gently to combine the juices, and cover. After 3 minutes, remove the lid and gently stir in the Salsa Verde until it's mixed in thoroughly with the clams and the liquid. Cover again and cook until the clams have opened, about 3 minutes more. Discard any that haven't opened after 5 minutes. Season with salt and pepper to taste.

3. Serve in bowls with grilled bread.

aarón's adobo

I want to tell you that no one can match Mexican cooks when it comes to meat. But when you've lived in the American South, you realize that for every phenomenal taqueria or market stall selling unbelievably tender pork or charred steak in my home country, there's a barbecue joint hawking equally amazing smoked pork shoulder or brisket below the Mason-Dixon Line.

In an effort to harness the awesomeness of both camps of carnivorous cooks, I created a fusion of the adobos of Mexico (pastes of chiles, garlic, and spices used to marinate meat) and the dry rubs dreamed up by barbecue pitmasters in the United States. But instead of making a paste, I stick to dried spices, even substituting powdered garlic and onion for the fresh stuff. That way, your blend will last for *months* if you store it in an airtight container in a cool, dry place. I use pasillas and anchos, two chiles common in Mexican cooking that are big on flavor, not fire. The result is smoky and sweet-smelling with a little heat and a backdrop of spices, and it all reinvigorates when the adobo-rubbed meat hits the grill.

aarón's adobo

MAKES ABOUT 1½ CUPS

¼ cup cumin seeds

¼ cup coriander seeds

¼ cup fennel seeds

¼ cup yellow mustard seeds

2 pasilla chiles, stemmed, seeded, deveined, and torn into small pieces

2 ancho chiles, stemmed, seeded, deveined, and torn into small pieces

½ cup dried whole oregano (preferably Mexican)

2 tablespoons onion powder

2 tablespoons garlic powder

¼ cup Spanish paprika (pimentón), preferably sweet or hot

1. Heat a dry skillet over medium-low heat. Pour in the cumin, coriander, fennel, and mustard seeds along with the pieces of pasilla and ancho chiles. Toast, stirring constantly, until it's very aromatic and just begins to smoke, about 3 minutes.

2. Dump the mixture onto a plate and let it cool to room temperature. Grind it to a fine powder in a spice grinder or clean coffee grinder.

3. Put the powder in a large bowl and add the oregano, onion powder, garlic powder, and paprika. Stir them really well to combine.

4. Store the adobo in an airtight container or resealable plastic bag in a cool, dark place for up to a month.

SIMPLE WAYS TO USE IT

- The big, bold flavors of this adobo make it a perfect partner for beef, pork, lamb, and duck.

- When I plan to serve fish, I'll often stir a little adobo into plain Greek yogurt, cover it and let it chill for an hour or so, then use it to top cooked salmon, sea bass, or bluefish.

- Toss chunks of sweet winter squash such as butternut or kabocha with oil and a tablespoon or so of the spice blend, then roast them.

- When you're cooking onions at the start of making stew or chili, stir in some of my adobo about a minute before your onions are fully browned. The spices get lively from the heat and improve whatever goes into the pot afterward.

- To give simple black bean soup a lift, stir in my adobo as it's simmering. Finish each bowl with a dollop of adobo-spiked sour cream.

ANCHO CHILES

When fresh poblano peppers (the mild, forest-green chiles) are dried, they become one of my favorite things in the world: anchos, which have a sweet, almost prunelike flavor (after all, they are dried fruits) with a smoky quality and a fleshy texture that I'm just in love with.

GOING WHOLE SPICE

There's absolutely nothing wrong with powdered dried spices. I use them sometimes, for sure. That said, I love buying whole spices—whole peppercorns, cumin and coriander seeds—and toasting and grinding them myself. Nothing beats the flavor or fragrance, and it barely takes any effort. Dump the spices into a skillet (nope, no oil necessary) that you've preheated over medium-low heat. Swirl, shake, stir, and toss those spices, and soon they'll start smelling so good you'll want to dive into the pan. Get yourself a spice grinder or coffee grinder (just not one you actually use for grinding coffee), turn them into a powder, and get ready for better-tasting food.

THE REPLACEMENTS

Let me ask you something about your cumin. How long has that little jar been hanging out in your cupboard, slowly becoming better and better at approximating sawdust? Spices might last forever, but their flavor doesn't. So get into the habit of scribbling a little date on your bags and jars and replacing them every six months. And if you're fretting about having to throw away what's left, start cooking with spices more often! Then you won't have anything left to chuck.

MEXICAN OREGANO

This herb is near and dear to my heart. When I was growing up, I'd visit my family's cattle ranch in Chihuahua, Mexico, where the cows grazed on wild oregano. And I swear that when my grandfather served us steaks made from his animals, I'd taste a perfumey whiff of it. I can't tell you how many times I've sat down to a bowl of pozole (hearty hominy soup) and sprinkled on the Mexican oregano that so often comes alongside, inhaling deeply as the dried herb hit the hot soup and sent up its scent.

People often ask me why they should go out of their way to find it, why it's special, why I'd trade all the Greek and Italian oregano in the world for a teaspoon of the Mexican stuff. My answer: Crush some between your fingers and find out for yourself. You can find dried Mexican oregano at any Mexican grocery store, in the spice aisle in many supermarkets, or online (see Resources, page 185). But if you really have to, you can substitute dried marjoram.

churrasco with open fire–roasted vegetable salsa

Cooking over fire makes everything so tasty that you don't have to do much. So I keep it super simple here, rubbing steak with my adobo and serving it with a chunky salsa of charred vegetables. The prep's easy, the cooking's easy, but wait until you taste the result. If you want an extra jolt of flavor, serve some Salsa Verde (page 20) on the side.

SERVES 4

6 tablespoons olive oil

2 garlic cloves, thinly sliced

2 medium red onions, halved

4 plum tomatoes, halved and cored

1 jalapeño or ½ serrano chile, stemmed (yup, seeds too, if you can take the heat)

1 medium zucchini, quartered lengthwise, seeds scraped out

1 medium leek, root trimmed but left intact, quartered lengthwise and well rinsed

1 red bell pepper, stemmed, seeded, and sliced

Salt and freshly ground black pepper

Four 8-ounce pieces beef tenderloin (see Note) or skirt steak

¼ cup Aarón's Adobo (page 32)

2 tablespoons thinly sliced fresh basil leaves

1. Combine the olive oil and garlic in a small skillet and set the pan over medium heat. Cook, stirring often, until the garlic is brown but not burned, about 3 minutes. Take the pan off the heat and let the garlic cool to room temperature in the oil, then discard the garlic; it has done its work!

2. Preheat a grill to high or heat a dry grill pan over medium-high heat.

3. Combine the onions, tomatoes, jalapeño, zucchini, leek, and red pepper in a large mixing bowl, pour half of the garlic oil on top, and toss well. Season generously with salt and pepper. Grill the vegetables until they're soft and a little bit charred, turning once. Return the vegetables to the mixing bowl to cool as you grill the steak.

4. Season each steak with salt and 1 tablespoon of the adobo and rub it with some of the remaining garlic oil. Grill the meat for 4 to 5 minutes per side for medium-rare. Transfer the steaks to a platter to rest.

5. Transfer the grilled vegetables to a cutting board and coarsely chop them into bite-size pieces. Put them back in the bowl and toss them with the remaining garlic oil and the basil. Season with salt and pepper to taste.

6. Put the meat on serving plates and spoon the vegetable salsa on top. Serve right away.

NOTE: Ask your butcher to cut the tenderloin pieces in a ½-inch-thick spiral so you can open them up and lay them out flat.

grilled pork tenderloin with aarón's adobo

It doesn't get simpler than this. You rub on the adobo, let those flavors sink in for half an hour, and get that meat to the heat! Even if you don't have a grill, the smoky spices will give you a taste of outdoor cooking. If you're feeling ambitious, whip up my Smoky Black Bean Sauce (page 16) or spoon on easy and amazing Roasted Tomatillo Salsa (page 78).

SERVES 4

1 tablespoon olive oil

One 1½-pound pork tenderloin

¼ cup Aarón's Adobo (page 32)

1. Rub the olive oil all over the tenderloin, then pat on the adobo. Set the tenderloin aside to marinate for 30 minutes.

2. Meanwhile, preheat the grill to high or preheat the broiler.

3. Generously season the pork with salt, then grill on all sides until an instant-read thermometer inserted into the center registers 145°F, 15 to 20 minutes. Let the pork rest for 5 minutes before slicing.

banging baby's-got-back ribs

My strategy with ribs? Load on the flavor. First, these baby backs get a spice massage, which really gets things popping. Next I whip up a crazy-good sweet and tangy sauce while the pork's cooking and lay it on at the end, just before the ribs are done, so the heat makes it all bubbly and sticky. A charcoal grill will add even more tastiness, but I've added so much already that you're good even if you use a gas grill or your oven.

SERVES 6 (HALF A RACK PER PERSON)

3 racks (about 5 pounds) baby back pork ribs

1 cup Aarón's Adobo (page 32)

3 tablespoons extra virgin olive oil

2 medium white or yellow onions, finely chopped

4 garlic cloves, very finely chopped

½ teaspoon cayenne pepper

2 cups Chile Colorado Sauce (page 134)

One 15-ounce can crushed tomatoes

½ cup molasses

½ cup apple cider vinegar

Grated zest and juice of 1 orange

1. At least 8 hours before you plan to cook, lay the ribs on a cutting board, curved bone side up. Using a sharp paring knife, slice into the tough white membrane covering the ribs. Carefully peel off and discard the membrane. Rub the ribs generously all over with the adobo. Wrap them in plastic wrap and refrigerate them for at least 8 hours, or overnight, to allow the flavors to penetrate.

2. Make the sauce. Heat the olive oil in a large saucepan over medium heat. Add the onions and garlic and cook them until softened and translucent, about 6 minutes. Add the cayenne, Chile Colorado Sauce, tomatoes, molasses, vinegar, and orange zest and juice and bring the mixture to a boil. Reduce the heat and simmer, stirring occasionally, until reduced and thick, about 45 minutes.

3. When you're ready to cook, preheat a gas grill to medium or an oven to 250°F, or burn down charcoal to red embers covered with gray ash. Turn off one burner or push the coals to one side and put the ribs on the grill rack over indirect heat. Cover the grill and cook the ribs for 2 hours, adding more charcoal now and then as necessary to keep the heat even. For oven cooking, line a baking sheet with aluminum foil and lay the ribs on it. Mop them thickly with the sauce, and cover with more foil. Roast for 2 to 3 hours, adding more sauce every 30 minutes, until the meat is tender and falling off the bone. (Times will vary; check the meat every 30 minutes.)

4. For grilling, after 2 hours, brush the ribs thickly with the sauce on both sides and flip them. Cover the grill and cook, brushing occasionally with sauce, until the ribs are tender, about 30 minutes more.

5. Serve warm or at room temperature with any extra sauce for dipping.

cilantro-cotija pesto

I was sitting in a tiny Italian restaurant in Manhattan, elbow to elbow with strangers and eating pasta with the best freaking pesto I've ever had, when it hit me: *What if I swapped the pine nuts in the classic pesto for pumpkin seeds, the rich and delicious addition to so many Mexican sauces? That'd be tasty*, I thought, as I took another bite. Or maybe I'd sub cotija cheese for the Parmesan. I took another bite, trying to focus on those awesome noodles, but now my mind was spinning out of control. *I'll add cilantro along with the basil! I'll toss in a little chile!* This is what happens when a Mexican chef spends twenty-plus years living in New York: he gets CADD (culinary attention deficit disorder).

But let me brag for a second and tell you that after I finished my pasta, popped into a grocery store on my way home, and gave my blender a workout, I had a new kind of pesto that tasted amazing—it turns out that cilantro and basil go together like ice cream and apple pie—and has been a staple in my kitchen ever since.

cilantro-cotija pesto

MAKES 2 CUPS

1 cup unsalted raw or roasted pumpkin
   seeds

½ bunch fresh cilantro, stems trimmed
   2 inches from the bottom

1 cup fresh basil leaves

1 cup olive oil, plus extra for storage

½ serrano chile or 1 jalapeño, coarsely
   chopped (yup, seeds too, if you can
   take the heat)

2 garlic cloves, coarsely chopped

½ cup crumbled cotija (preferably the
   Cacique brand) or shredded pecorino
   or Parmesan

Salt and freshly ground black pepper

1. Preheat the oven to 400°F.

2. Spread the pumpkin seeds in an even layer
on a dry baking sheet. Put the sheet in the
oven and bake, checking them and shaking
the pan every 3 minutes, until they start to
dance, puff up, and brown lightly, about
10 minutes. Take the pan out of the oven,
transfer the seeds to a bowl, and let cool to
room temperature.

3. Put the cilantro, basil, and olive oil into a
food processor and puree for 2 minutes. Add
the chile, garlic, pumpkin seeds, and cotija, and
pulse until you have a coarse puree. Season
with salt and pepper to taste. To store, put it
into a container with a tight-fitting lid and pour
¼ inch of olive oil over the surface to keep
out the air. Each time you use it, stir that oil in,
and replace with another ¼ inch of oil before
closing the container. This makes an airtight seal
that will keep it tasting fresh for up to 10 days.

SIMPLE WAYS TO USE IT

- Treat it like traditional pesto and toss it with al dente pasta cooked in plenty of well-salted water. Add a touch of the cooking water to the sauced noodles right before you serve them so they're not too dry, and grate some extra cotija on top.

- Add it to a hearty summer vegetable salad—say, juicy tomatoes, grilled corn cut from the cob, and crunchy green beans—and you're golden. I'd also eat the heck out of potato salad dressed with this green love instead of mayo.

- Scallops, fish fillets, and chicken breasts are just begging you to mix this pesto with butter and perch a hunk of it on top during the last minute or two of cooking.

PUMPKIN SEEDS

You know those white pumpkin seeds that are often roasted, salted, and scarfed as a snack? That's *not* what Mexicans use when they cook. Instead, my recipe calls for raw hulled pumpkin seeds, which are smaller and pale green. You can find them at just about any natural food store if they're not at your local supermarket near the nuts.

If you can only find pumpkin seeds that are already roasted, no problem. In fact, it means you can skip the step of roasting the seeds in the recipe. Still, I prefer doing this myself, because it's as easy as turning on the oven—you can even roast them the day before—and because you almost always get a better result when you do things yourself. If you can only find them salted, you're still not out of luck—just wipe some of the salt off with a paper towel and be extra careful when you season with salt after blending.

COTIJA CHEESE

You might have had this tasty Mexican cow's milk cheese the last time you bit into a tostada or one of those fabulous ears of corn slathered with mayo and squirted with lime juice. It has the crumbly, grate-able texture of Parmesan, but it's got a bit of funk to it, like me. I love the cotija made by Cacique, which has been making Mexican cheese in the United States for forty years and knows its stuff. If you have to, you can substitute aged Manchego, Parmesan, pecorino, or, really, any dry sharp cheese.

TRICK: KEEPING YOUR PESTO GREEN

This pesto's the bomb because it tastes great, but also because of its stunning color. It's so green it looks like you blended together a whole field of grass, a summer garden, and Kermit the Frog. At least until air comes along and messes everything up. The chemical reaction that occurs when air hits the basil is called oxidation, but all you need to know is that it can turn your pesto brownish—and fast. You have four options to prevent it. The first is to make your pesto right before you serve it. But if you make it more than ten minutes before that:

- Pour a little bit of olive oil over the top. It'll spread out and make a sort of force field to prevent air from hitting the basil.

- Cover it with plastic wrap and make sure you press the plastic against the surface of the pesto.

- Mix in a little magic dust—I mean, vitamin C powder, which you'll find at any health food store.

MOVE OVER, BLENDER

I'm not going to tell you that you can't make pesto in a blender. But I will urge you to do it in a food processor. While the blender liquefies your ingredients, the food processor leaves you with this beautiful coarse puree, with the ingredients unified but still hanging on to a little of their own identities. The blades will also catch the ingredients easily. In a blender, you might have to add water, which is fine but dilutes the flavor. If you don't have a food processor, use a mortar and pestle. If you don't have a mortar and pestle, then use the blender. I won't be mad at you.

blue potatoes
with cilantro-cotija pesto

I love the combination of tender potatoes and crisp green beans. Yeah, you could drizzle them with olive oil and sprinkle on some salt and be good to go. But if you have my Cilantro-Cotija Pesto at the ready, you can blast them with flavor and turn a decent side into a memorable one.

SERVES 4 TO 6

1 pound blue fingerling potatoes or regular
    fingerling potatoes

Salt

1 pound slender green beans, trimmed and
    cut into 2-inch pieces

½ cup Cilantro-Cotija Pesto (page 42), or
    more to taste

1. Put the potatoes in a large heavy saucepan and cover them with cold water. Add 1 teaspoon salt. Bring to a boil and cook just until the potatoes are tender and easily pierced with a fork, 10 to 12 minutes. Drain the potatoes, rinse them under cool water, and put them in a large serving bowl.

2. While the potatoes are cooking, bring another large saucepan of lightly salted water to a boil, then add the beans. Cook for 4 to 5 minutes, until they're just crisp and still bright green. Drain them, then rinse under cold running water to stop the cooking.

3. Add the beans to the potatoes in the bowl and spoon on the Cilantro-Cotija Pesto, tossing gently to coat and being careful not to break up the potatoes. Serve at room temperature.

chiles rellenos
with vegetable picadillo

Poblano chiles deserve way more love than they get. When they're cooked they have such an awesome smoky, slightly sweet flavor. There's nothing quite like it. I love stuffing them, because it gives them a chance to be the star. For the bomb presentation, pour a pool of Smoky Black Bean Sauce (page 16) onto each plate and put a stuffed chile on top.

SERVES 4 AS AN APPETIZER

4 large poblano chiles

1 tablespoon canola oil

¼ cup finely chopped white onion

¼ cup finely chopped red bell pepper

¼ cup corn kernels, fresh or frozen

2 tablespoons chopped fresh cilantro

½ cup diced queso blanco (preferably the Cacique brand) or Jack cheese

1 tablespoon Cilantro-Cotija Pesto (page 42)

1. Turn two of your stove's burners to medium-high. Place 2 poblano chiles on each burner and roast them, turning them occasionally with tongs, until they're charred all over and soft but not mushy, about 7 minutes. Transfer them to a big bowl or soup pot, cover it tightly with plastic wrap, and let the chiles steam for 10 minutes. Peel them, being careful to keep them intact. Rub off the skins; don't rinse under water.

2. Preheat the oven to 350°F. Heat the oil in a skillet over medium heat. Add the onion, bell pepper, and corn and cook until the onion has softened and the pepper is just cooked through, about 5 minutes. Stir in the cilantro and transfer the mixture to a large bowl to cool slightly. Add the cheese and Cilantro-Cotija Pesto and mix well.

3. Cut a lengthwise slit in each pepper, pull out and discard the seeds and veins, but keep the stem on. Divide the filling among the chiles. Lay them in a 1-quart baking dish and bake for 10 to 12 minutes, until the cheese is melting. Serve at once.

NOTE: If you don't have a gas stove, put your peppers on a baking sheet and cook them under the broiler until they char, turning several times, about 10 minutes all together.

calabacitas con queso

Ditch the same old sautéed zucchini (*calabacitas* is Spanish for "little squash") for this lively dish that takes full advantage of my funky Mexican pesto, with its whack of cilantro and touch of spice. Make sure the zucchini retains a little of its crunchy texture, and you're a happy camper.

SERVES 4

2 tablespoons extra virgin olive oil

1 garlic clove, very finely chopped

1 pound zucchini, cut into large dice

1 large tomato, cored, seeded, and diced

1 scallion, thinly sliced

1 tablespoon Cilantro-Cotija Pesto (page 42)

½ cup crumbled queso blanco (preferably the Cacique brand) or lightly salty feta

Freshly squeezed lime juice

Salt and freshly ground black pepper

1. Put the olive oil and garlic in a large skillet and set it over medium heat. Once the garlic begins to sizzle, cook, stirring, for 1 minute so the oil gets some of that garlic flavor. Add the zucchini and cook, stirring occasionally, until the zucchini has softened slightly, about 3 minutes. Add the tomato and scallion and cook until the tomato begins to break down, about 5 minutes.

2. Take the skillet off the heat and stir in the Cilantro-Cotija Pesto and queso blanco until the cheese starts to melt. Season with lime juice, salt, and pepper to taste, and serve.

roasted tomato–chile de árbol salsa

This is it, my quintessential red salsa. It's what every taqueria in my fantasy would set out in little bowls. It's what everyone on earth would whip up instead of buying jarred salsa in stores. But here's something to get excited about: you can use this sauce as so much more than just a taco topper.

The fun begins with juicy ripe tomatoes that get charred and sweet in your oven. Lightly caramelized onion and garlic add even more sweetness and flavor. Then there are the dried chiles de árbol, which infuse that sweetness with mouth-thrilling heat but nothing that'll send you running for a glass of milk.

roasted tomato–chile de árbol salsa

MAKES 2 CUPS

1 pound plum tomatoes (about 4)

3 to 6 chiles de árbol, depending on how spicy you like it

2 tablespoons olive oil

1 medium white onion, chopped

4 garlic cloves, crushed

½ cup chopped fresh cilantro

1 teaspoon salt

½ teaspoon freshly ground black pepper

1. Preheat the broiler.

2. Put the tomatoes on a baking sheet and broil, turning occasionally, until the tomatoes are nice and charred, 10 to 12 minutes. Take the tomatoes out, let them cool just until you can handle them, slip off the skins, and cut out the tough cores. Transfer the tomatoes to a big bowl (don't you dare forget the tomato juice that has leaked out and reduced to awesomeness on the baking sheet), then roughly chop them.

3. While the tomatoes are broiling, heat a dry skillet over medium heat and toast the chiles (in batches, if necessary), flipping them over occasionally, until they just begin to smoke, about 5 minutes. Set them aside in a bowl.

4. Put the olive oil, onion, and garlic in a saucepan, set it over medium heat, and cook, stirring occasionally, until the onion is soft, about 7 minutes. Add the toasted chiles, tomatoes, and 2 cups water, bring to a simmer, and cook for about 12 minutes, so the flavors come together. Let it cool a bit.

5. Carefully transfer the mixture to a blender. Add the cilantro, salt, and pepper and puree until the mixture is very smooth.

6. Pour the mixture through a medium-mesh sieve into a bowl. Serve at room temperature or slightly chilled.

7. Store the salsa in the refrigerator, tightly covered, for up to a week, or in the freezer for a month.

SIMPLE WAYS TO USE IT

- Next time you sauté zucchini, give it some Mexican flavor by adding a tablespoon or two of this salsa, a bit of oregano, and grated cheese.

- Instead of a typical tomato sauce, add this spicy salsa to cooked pasta for a new take on the Italian arrabbiata. Parmesan works beautifully on top, but why not give cotija cheese a chance?

- Thin the salsa with a little stock and you have a high-octane liquid that you can use to braise bone-in chicken thighs, chunks of beef, or pork spareribs.

- Itching for incredible pico de gallo? Dice some fresh tomatoes and red onions, then add a few spoonfuls of this lip-tingling cooked salsa and a shower of chopped cilantro.

- Warm shredded leftover chicken in the salsa and you have a perfect partner for rice and beans or a fine filling for flautas, tamales, or empanadas.

TOMATOES

Do me a favor, okay? Don't use those rock-hard pinkish tomatoes you see in supermarkets, especially during the winter, for this recipe. You know what? Don't use them—ever. You'll get an infinitely better result, with all the red tomato love you expect, if you roast ripe, juicy ones. Actually, this is a great way to use those guys that are so ripe they're almost bursting. I suggest using plum tomatoes for this recipe because they roast quickly and taste great, but you should use the ripest tomatoes you can get your mitts on. Just know that large ones will take a little more time to cook fully. When I do find sexy ripe summer tomatoes, I buy a lot, roast them in a big batch, skin them, and freeze them in little portions in freezer bags so I'm ready to make salsa throughout the cold months. And finally, if you really can't find ripe tomatoes, drain a 28-ounce can of whole tomatoes that are labeled "fire-roasted"—those are actually pretty tasty.

CHILES DE ÁRBOL

I'll do anything—walk on hot coals, eat a habanero in one bite, give up tacos for a year (okay, that's going a bit far)—to get you to try dried chiles de árbol. If this slender chile had a fan club, I'd be the president. It's got some kick-you-in-the-mouth heat, but a ton of sharp, bright flavor, too. When I toast it in a pan, I always take a few careful sniffs, because the inviting, nutty aroma is like nothing else on earth.

As with all dried chiles, the best are the whole, stems-on guys that are supple, not dry and crumbly. If you've searched high and low and still can't find them (and, for some reason, don't want to order them online with a few clicks—see Resources, page 185), you can substitute the more common dried cayenne chiles. Even a teaspoon of ground cayenne, hot paprika, or hot (not sweet) pimentón will give you something tasty.

STORAGE

This salsa will keep for a week in the fridge and up to a few months in the freezer.

STRAINING

There are a lot of ways Mexican cooks would make sure that a salsa like this would be really silky, smooth, and free of little bits of chile and tomato skin. But not many of them would do what I suggest: straining it. Sure, you peel the skins from the tomatoes, though I swear the chile de árbol skin wouldn't break down completely even if you had a fancy professional blender with a nuclear reactor attached. And anyway, straining is so easy. After you've pureed the ingredients together, you pour the mixture into a medium-mesh sieve set over a bowl. After a little pushing and prodding with a spoon, the awesome, flavorful, silky stuff goes into the bowl and the skins and tough bits stay behind.

chicken tostadas

Ever wonder how the stewed chicken piled on top of the crunchy tortillas known as tostadas gets to be so damn delicious? Now you know—it's as easy as simmering it with salsa. Add refried beans, crunchy radishes and lettuce, and a bunch of other good stuff, and these will be snatched up by party guests before you can say *"¡Que rico!"* Or be selfish and treat them as an informal dinner for two.

**SERVES 6 AS AN APPETIZER
OR 2 AS A MAIN**

2 cups Roasted Tomato–Chile de Árbol
    Salsa (page 52)

3 cups shredded cooked chicken

Salt

One 16-ounce can refried beans

Vegetable oil, for frying

6 corn tortillas

1 Hass avocado

3 cups finely shredded iceberg lettuce

½ cup thinly sliced radishes

⅓ cup crumbled dry cheese, such as cotija
    (preferably the Cacique brand), lightly
    salty feta, or ricotta salata

½ cup crema fresca (preferably the Cacique
    brand) or sour cream

2 tablespoons chopped fresh cilantro

1 lime, cut into 6 wedges

1. Heat the Roasted Tomato–Chile de Árbol Salsa and chicken in a skillet or medium saucepan over medium heat, stirring occasionally, until the mixture is warmed through. Season with salt to taste, and keep it warm on the back of the stove.

2. Heat the refried beans in a small saucepan until hot. Set aside and keep warm.

3. Line a baking sheet with paper towels. Pour ¼ inch of oil into a medium cast-iron skillet and heat over medium-high heat. Put 1 tortilla in the oil and fry until golden brown, turning once and pushing it flat into the hot oil, about 1 minute total. Transfer the fried tortilla to the baking sheet to drain. Repeat with the remaining tortillas.

4. Carefully spread a layer of refried beans on each tortilla with a knife, then spoon on some of the chicken mixture. Halve, pit, peel, and slice the avocado and top each tostada with avocado, lettuce, and radishes. Sprinkle each with cheese, then drizzle on the crema fresca or top with a dollop of sour cream. Garnish with the cilantro and serve immediately with a wedge of lime on the side to squeeze on before eating.

crab tostadas

One of the many treats in the markets of Mexico that I crave is the tostada, a crispy tortilla piled with anything from chicken in mole to tender chunks of octopus. I especially love when it's topped with sweet, delicate crab, and this dead-simple rendition, made extra lively by my Roasted Tomato–Chile de Árbol Salsa, is full of that market flavor.

MAKES 6 TOSTADAS

½ pound fresh Dungeness crabmeat or jumbo lump crab

⅓ cup crema fresca (preferably the Cacique brand) or crème fraîche (see Note)

¼ cup finely chopped fresh chives

¼ teaspoon ground white pepper

Juice of ½ lime (about 1 tablespoon)

1 tablespoon Roasted Tomato–Chile de Árbol Salsa (page 52)

Salt

6 tostadas, purchased or homemade (see page 55, step 3)

Cilantro leaves, picked off their stems, for garnish

1. Put the crabmeat in a bowl and pick over it carefully, removing any bits of shell. Flake it gently with a fork to break up the biggest chunks, but don't mash it into a paste. Gently fold in the crema fresca, chives, pepper, lime juice, and Roasted Tomato–Chile de Árbol Salsa. Season with salt to taste. (If you're not using it right away, cover tightly with plastic wrap and chill for up to 2 hours. Bring it to room temperature and stir gently before serving.)

2. To serve, divide the crab mixture among the tostadas and garnish with fresh cilantro leaves. (If you like, you can make mini tostadas. Cut regular-size tortillas into a few little circles: invert a cup and trace around it with a knife.)

NOTE: If you can't find either crema fresca or crème fraîche, make your own! The day before you begin this recipe, whisk together ⅓ cup heavy cream with 2 tablespoons sour cream. Cover the surface with plastic wrap and let it sit at room temperature for 8 hours or overnight, until the cream thickens.

sopa seca *mexican-style pasta*

Pasta. That's not Mexican, right? Think again. You see it in homes throughout Mexico, one of the many foreign foods that we have welcomed into our cuisine and something I ate growing up. We call this Mexican comfort food, funnily enough, *sopa seca*, which means "dry soup." Of course, we give it a Latin twist, subbing cilantro for basil, cotija or queso fresco for Parmesan, and spice for subtlety.

SERVES 2 AS A SIDE OR SNACK

¼ cup canola oil

1 cup small shaped pasta such as melon seeds, orzo, or alphabets

½ cup Roasted Tomato–Chile de Árbol Salsa (page 52)

2 cups chicken stock (low-sodium store-bought is fine)

1 tablespoon chopped fresh cilantro

A handful of shredded cotija or queso fresco (preferably the Cacique brand), or pecorino, Parmesan, or lightly salty feta

1. Heat the oil in a Dutch oven or medium pot over medium-high heat until it ripples. Add the pasta and cook, stirring constantly, until the pasta is golden, about 3 minutes.

2. Scoop out and discard 2 tablespoons of the oil. Add the Roasted Tomato–Chile de Árbol Salsa and cook for 2 minutes, stirring the whole time. Pour in the chicken stock and let the liquid come to a simmer. Cover the pot and cook, stirring once in a while, until the liquid is absorbed and the pasta is tender, about 20 minutes.

3. Divide the pasta between two bowls and garnish with the cilantro and cheese.

sopes with huitlacoche or wild mushrooms

Some of my favorite places to eat in Mexico are the markets, where there are often entire sections devoted to little eateries called fondas. And though I love to hunker down in front of a steaming bowl of pozole, I usually head straight to the stalls selling *sopes*. Think of them as slightly thicker tortillas cooked in a little oil and topped with unbelievably tasty stuff. My topping of choice is huitlacoche, the corn fungus whose English translation does no justice to its sophisticated, mushroomy flavor. (If you just winced, you might want to substitute an assortment of wild mushrooms.) The crisp-soft texture of the tortilla, the huitlacoche, salty bits of cheese, a cool drizzle of cream—the only thing that could improve on this combo is my Roasted Tomato–Chile de Árbol Salsa.

SERVES 4 AS AN APPETIZER

1 cup masa harina (corn tortilla flour; see Resources, page 185)

¾ cup warm water

About ¼ cup vegetable oil

1 teaspoon very finely chopped garlic (about 2 medium cloves)

1 medium white onion, finely chopped

1 teaspoon finely chopped serrano chile or 2 teaspoons finely chopped jalapeño (yup, seeds too, if you can take the heat)

One 16-ounce can or two 7.6-ounce cans huitlacoche, drained, or ½ pound mixed wild mushrooms, coarsely chopped

Salt

2 tablespoons chopped fresh cilantro

About ¾ cup Roasted Tomato–Chile de Árbol Salsa (page 52)

3 tablespoons crema fresca (preferably the Cacique brand) or crème fraîche thinned with a little water

A few small handfuls of crumbled queso fresco (preferably the Cacique brand)

1. Put the tortilla flour in a large bowl, pour in the water, and get in there with your hands, kneading until you have a uniform dough. It should take only a minute or two. You want a nice, moist dough, so work in a little more warm water if it's dry. If it's sticky, work in a little more tortilla flour.

2. Break the dough into four equal pieces and roll each one into a ball. Put the balls on a plate or cutting board and cover them with plastic wrap to keep the dough from drying out. One at a time, roll them out with a rolling pin or clean wine bottle until they're thin circles, about ¼ inch thick.

3. Preheat the oven to 200°F and line a baking sheet with paper towels.

4. Brush a little of the oil on a skillet or a *comal* and heat it over medium-high heat until it's good and hot. Carefully add the first *sope* and cook it for 45 seconds, or until little brown blisters appear on the bottom. Flip it over with a spatula and cook for another 30 to 45 seconds. Flip it over again, count to 10, and transfer to the baking sheet. Keep it warm in the oven. Repeat with the remaining 3 *sopes* (adding a little more oil if you need to) and keep them in the oven until you're ready to serve them.

5. Pour a couple of tablespoons of the oil into a skillet and add the garlic, onion, and chile. Set the skillet over medium heat and cook, stirring occasionally, until the onion is soft, about 5 minutes. Add the huitlacoche or mushrooms along with a good pinch of salt and cook, stirring occasionally, until the huitlacoche is heated through, about 5 minutes, or until the mushrooms are a little browned and cooked through, about 10 minutes. Take the mixture off the heat and stir in the cilantro.

6. Arrange your *sopes* on a platter. Cover with a thin layer of Roasted Tomato–Chile de Árbol Salsa, the huitlacoche or mushrooms, and finally a drizzle of the crema fresca and a sprinkle of cheese. Serve the remaining salsa on the side in case your friends want more, which they will.

cemita sandwiches

Everyone in Puebla has strong opinions on where to get the best *cemita*, the state's deservedly famous overstuffed sandwich with its crusty namesake bread. "It's this market stall," one friend says. "Nope," says another, "it's that one." "Guys, guys," says a third buddy. "You've got the wrong market altogether." With this fantastic version, you'll be able to chime in and argue that the best one isn't at a market at all—it's at your house.

SERVES 4

One 1-pound pork tenderloin, cut into
    ½-inch-thick slices

Salt and freshly ground black pepper

1 teaspoon dried whole oregano (preferably
    Mexican), crumbled

1 teaspoon ground cumin

½ teaspoon ground cinnamon or 1 teaspoon
    canela (see page 104)

½ teaspoon cayenne pepper

About 3 tablespoons vegetable oil

4 Mexican *cemita* rolls or other large crusty
    rolls

2 ripe Hass avocados

Juice of ½ lime (about 1 tablespoon)

16 papalo leaves or ½ cup whole cilantro
    leaves (see Note)

4 slices ripe tomato

4 canned chipotles in adobo, finely chopped,
    or more to taste

4 thin slices white onion

One 8-ounce ball fresh mozzarella, pulled
    into shreds

½ cup Roasted Tomato–Chile de Árbol Salsa
    (page 52)

1. Preheat the oven to 200°F.

2. Put the pork slices between two sheets of plastic wrap and pound each with a meat mallet or a rolling pin until it is ¼ inch thick. Season the pieces generously with salt and pepper and sprinkle them with the oregano, cumin, cinnamon, and cayenne. Pour a couple of tablespoons of the oil into a large cast-iron skillet over medium-high heat. Add the pork, in batches, adding a little more oil as needed, and sear on both sides until just cooked through, 1 to 2 minutes per side. Transfer the pork to an ovenproof plate and keep it warm in the oven.

3. Slice open the rolls and toast or grill until golden.

4. Split open and pit the avocados, slice, and season with lime juice and salt. On the bottom half of each roll, layer the papalo leaves, pork, avocado, tomato, chipotles, onion, and mozzarella cheese. Drizzle on some Roasted Tomato–Chile de Árbol Salsa, add the top of the roll, and serve at once.

NOTE: What the heck is papalo? It's an herb that you really, really want to get to know. There's nothing quite like the thin, almost crunchy leaves that resemble little lily pads, with the pleasantly bitter flavor that tastes almost as if someone crammed the flavor of a whole bunch of cilantro into each little leaf. Look for bunches with bright green leaves and firm stems in some Mexican grocery stores. Cilantro makes a good substitute, but believe me, the joys of papalo are worth a little searching.

habanero love

While my Garlic-Chipotle Love (page 6) is a tribute to the smells and flavors I grew up with, this Habanero Love represents both my childhood and the places I've been since.

It features the habanero, pride of the Yucatán and the most misunderstood chile out there. It deserves its rep as one of the world's hottest chiles, but just as Mexican food has so much more to offer than tacos and enchiladas, the habanero has more to strut about than just its champion Scoville scale status. Peel back the curtain of heat to get a glimpse of the real show: the chile's amazing fruity, floral flavor.

This nod to my home country and my past mixes it up with my present. Nowadays I often look outside of Mexico for inspiration—to the rest of Latin America, the Caribbean, the United States, or wherever delicious ideas live. So while the habanero is the icing, the cake comes from places like Puerto Rico and Cuba, where people slowly cook peppers, onions, and garlic together in oil to bring out their natural sugars. The sweet, sweet goodness you're left with is called *sofrito*, and I've been making it for more than a decade. It's the flavor foundation of so many Latin dishes, even if you don't know it's in there. Whenever you've eaten a stew or bowl of beans and thought, *Damn, that's good!*, you just know the cook started with a fine *sofrito*.

Blend it all together and you have a gorgeous orange-red puree with big flavor and lip-tingling heat that you'll employ more often than a twenty-year-old uses a fake ID.

habanero love

½ cup olive oil

1 large red bell pepper, chopped

1 large yellow bell pepper, chopped

1 large red onion, chopped

2 medium carrots, chopped

4 garlic cloves, sliced

Salt

1 habanero or Scotch bonnet chile, very finely chopped (yup, seeds too, if you can take the heat)

1. Heat a large saucepan over medium heat. Pour in the olive oil and add the bell peppers, onion, carrots, and garlic. Add a good sprinkle of salt and cook, stirring occasionally, until the vegetables have all softened, about 20 minutes.

2. Stir in the habanero and cook for 5 minutes more. Let the mixture cool to room temperature.

3. Transfer it to a blender, along with ½ cup water. Work in batches, if necessary. Blend until the Habanero Love is very smooth— Michael Jackson smooth. Store in a tightly covered container in the refrigerator for up to a week.

SIMPLE WAYS TO USE IT

- Whisk in some olive oil, add a little citrus for tartness or agave for sweetness, and you've got a dressing that'll improve any salad. Thanks to the habanero, it goes especially well in salads that feature fruit like mango slices or orange segments.

- It's got all the flavor of slow-cooked peppers and onions, so stir it into stews and chilis near the end of cooking to give them a little depth, sweetness, and fire.

- Turn it into habanero mayo: Whisk together 1 cup mayonnaise, ¼ cup Habanero Love, and the juice of 1 lime. Season with salt and pepper to taste, have a taste, and smile.

TAKE IT SLOW

Making *sofrito* is like charming a good woman—it's best if you do it slowly. It takes time to coax out all the awesome sweetness in those vegetables, which tames the intense heat of the habanero so its fruity flavor can shine. So here's the best advice you'll get all day: Don't rush your *sofrito*.

HABANERO CHILES

As anyone knows who has mistakenly rubbed their eyes after touching a habanero or accidentally chomped on too big a piece, these chiles are the culinary equivalent of plutonium—they are to be handled with great care. The same goes for the habanero's close relative, the Scotch bonnet chile. The same goes for both green (unripe) habaneros and yellow, orange, and red (ripe) ones. So please, don't be a hero. Wear gloves whenever you're dealing with them. And here's another tip: Don't hunch over them as you mince. Instead, keep your back nice and straight, so in case it spatters as you're chopping, your eyes will be far away.

GARLIC

Can I vent for a minute? Thank you. I've seen otherwise excellent cooks toss chopped garlic into a pan of hot oil. That's not how I roll. What happens is each piece quickly gets brown on the outside before the inside is cooked. By the time the inside loses its harsh raw flavor, the outside is black and bitter. Now, in this recipe, you're cool as long as you stir occasionally and keep the heat to medium. But here's a tip for any other time you're cooking garlic in oil: Pour some oil into your pan, add the garlic, and then put the pan on the heat. Tell your friends.

spicy chicken fricassee with hearty vegetables

A lot of the flavor in most stews comes from vegetables, slowly cooked to bring out their sweetness. My Habanero Love has all of that and a big bonus: that fruity heat from the namesake chile. Once you stir it into chicken stock, you have a braising liquid that turns chicken and hearty vegetables into a memorable stew, the perfect weeknight dinner.

SERVES 4 TO 6

2 tablespoons olive or corn oil

One 3- to 4-pound chicken, cut into 8 pieces

1 quart chicken stock (low-sodium store-bought is fine)

1 cup Habanero Love (page 68)

1 malanga, peeled and cut into small cubes

1 green (unripe) plantain, peeled and cut into small cubes

1 cup diced calabaza (from about ¼ of a large calabaza) or another winter squash like butternut

¼ cup chopped fresh cilantro, for garnish

1. Preheat the oven to 375°F.

2. In a large Dutch oven or ovenproof pot with a lid, heat the oil over medium-high heat. Brown the chicken pieces in batches (don't crowd the pot), about 6 minutes per batch, turning them occasionally. Transfer them to a plate as you finish.

3. Pour the chicken stock into the pot and bring it to a simmer. Scrape the bottom with a wooden spoon to release the browned bits, then stir in the Habanero Love. Add the chicken, the malanga, green plantain, and calabaza. Cover the pot and transfer to the oven.

4. Cook until the chicken is falling off the bone and the vegetables are tender, about 1 hour.

5. Serve garnished with chopped cilantro.

NOTE: I love the combination of malanga (a starchy tuber also called yautia), green plantain, and calabaza, but you can use any vegetables you want! You can substitute yam, potato, or rutabaga for the malanga. Just keep in mind that only super-starchy stuff needs the full hour in the oven. If you're substituting an ingredient like zucchini, don't add it until 20 minutes or so before the chicken is done.

seafood stew with nuts and coconut

This is my take on the Brazilian dish called *vatapa*, a thick stew made with coconut milk and nuts. My version is more souplike than the original, like a funky Latin bouillabaisse, because that's how I like it. It's also brimming with flavor, thanks to my (and now *your*) secret weapon: Habanero Love. White rice makes the perfect sauce-soaker-upper.

SERVES 4

2 cups well-stirred coconut milk

1 cup Habanero Love (page 68)

1 cup homemade or store-bought fish stock or bottled clam juice

½ cup cashew nuts, finely chopped

½ cup blanched almonds, finely chopped

One 8- to 10-ounce sea bass fillet, cut into 4 pieces

1 pound medium shrimp, peeled and deveined

¼ cup chopped fresh cilantro

Salt

Thinly sliced fresh chile, for garnish

Steamed white rice, for serving

1 lime, quartered, for serving

1. Combine the coconut milk, Habanero Love, fish stock, cashews, and almonds in a large saucepan and bring to a simmer over medium heat. Cook, stirring occasionally, for 10 minutes.

2. Add the fish, lower the heat, and cook for 4 minutes, until the fish is white and opaque. (If you want a browned edge, sear the fish in a hot skillet over medium-high heat for 2 to 3 minutes, until the edges are crisped and browned, then add the fish to the hot broth.) Add the shrimp and cilantro. Cook until the fish and shrimp are just cooked through, about 4 minutes more. Season to taste with salt.

3. Garnish with slices of fresh chile, and serve right away in bowls with white rice and lime wedges.

scallop and shrimp ceviche

Latin America's ceviche obsession has taken hold here in the United States, and this version will show you exactly why. Fresh seafood marinated in tart, citrusy liquid is one of the most fun, refreshing ways to begin a dinner party.

SERVES 4 TO 6

½ cup Habanero Love (page 68)

2 tablespoons mango puree (see page 125)

⅓ cup freshly squeezed orange juice

¼ cup freshly squeezed lime juice, plus
    more as needed

2 tablespoons finely chopped red onion

2 tablespoons finely chopped seeded tomato

2 tablespoons chopped fresh cilantro

Salt

1 pound shrimp, peeled, deveined, and
    halved lengthwise

½ pound bay scallops, or ½ pound sea
    scallops cut into small pieces

Plantain or tortilla chips, for serving

1. Whisk together the Habanero Love, mango puree, orange juice, and lime juice in a large bowl. Add the onion, tomato, and cilantro, stir well, and set aside.

2. Prepare a big bowl of ice water. Bring a big pot of salted water to a simmer.

3. Add the shrimp to the simmering water and cook, stirring occasionally, just until they're cooked through, 45 seconds or so. Use a skimmer or slotted spoon to remove the shrimp and drop them into the bowl of ice water to stop the cooking.

4. Bring the water back to a simmer and cook the scallops, stirring occasionally, until they're just cooked through, about 45 seconds. Scoop them out and drop them into the ice water to stop the cooking.

5. Drain the shrimp and scallops really well and pat them dry with paper towels. Add them to the Habanero Love mixture. Stir well, cover the bowl with plastic wrap, and stick the bowl in the fridge for 1 hour.

6. When you're ready to serve it, season with salt and lime juice to taste. Serve with plantain or tortilla chips.

bacalaitos *codfish fritters with habanero mayo*

It's amazing that something as humble and inexpensive as salt cod could turn into such an impressive appetizer. Add habanero-spiked mayo that could make an old boot taste great, and watch how fast these crispy fritters disappear.

MAKES 16 FRITTERS

½ pound salt cod

6 cups milk

1½ cups all-purpose flour

1 teaspoon baking powder

1 small red onion, cut into ½-inch pieces

1 roasted red pepper (see Note, page 13), cut into ½-inch pieces

2 garlic cloves, finely chopped

½ bunch fresh cilantro, the root end trimmed by 3 inches and chopped

Vegetable oil, for frying

Habanero mayonnaise (see page 69), for serving

1. Soak the cod overnight in the refrigerator in 3 cups milk.

2. Drain the cod and discard the milk. Place the fish in a medium pot with the remaining 3 cups milk and 3 cups water. Bring to a boil over medium-high heat and cook until the fish is tender, 20 to 30 minutes.

3. Drain the fish, shred it into small pieces with two forks, and set it aside to cool to room temperature.

4. Preheat the oven to 200°F. In a large bowl, whisk together the flour, baking powder, and 1½ cups water to make a batter. Add the fish, onion, roasted pepper, garlic, and cilantro, and stir to combine.

5. Line a baking sheet with a few layers of paper towels.

6. Heat 1½ inches of oil in a large heavy pot over medium-high heat until it's 350°F (use a deep-fry thermometer). Working in batches, scoop out rounded tablespoons of the fritter batter and carefully ease them into the oil. Fry, turning each fritter once, until they're golden on the outside, about 5 minutes total. As they're finished, use a slotted spoon to transfer them to the paper towels to drain and keep them warm in the low oven. Let the oil heat up again before you fry the next batch.

7. Serve the fritters on a platter or in a bowl with a bowl of habanero mayonnaise on the side.

roasted tomatillo salsa

You see it in taquerias on winding side streets. It's in fondas, the little food stalls in markets where blue-collar folks get their chow on, and on dining room tables in homes across Mexico. It looks inconspicuous enough, just green salsa in a little dish. But I've seen giddy grown-ups go gaga over this ridiculously tasty stuff, like kids do over ice cream.

My version builds on the best of the traditional salsa. Instead of boiling the tomatillos, I roast them to intensify their flavor. A punch of chile and a fresh wallop of cilantro make this sauce sing like ten mariachis with megaphones.

Of course, you can spoon some thrillingly tangy tomatillo salsa over a nice steak or beans and rice and call it a day. But the fun doesn't stop there. In fact, that's just where it begins.

roasted tomatillo salsa

MAKES ABOUT 3 CUPS

1½ pounds fresh tomatillos

5 fresh serrano or 10 jalapeño chiles,
   stemmed (yup, seeds too, if you can
   take the heat)

3 whole garlic cloves, peeled

1 large white onion, peeled and sliced
   ½ inch thick

¼ cup olive oil

Kosher salt

½ cup chopped fresh cilantro

Freshly ground black pepper

1. Preheat the broiler. Remove the husks from
the tomatillos. Rinse the tomatillos under
warm water to remove the stickiness. Dry
them with a paper towel.

2. Put the tomatillos, chiles, garlic, and onion
on a baking sheet. Drizzle them with the olive
oil and sprinkle on 2 teaspoons or so of kosher
salt. Broil them a few inches from the heat,
turning everything once, until the tomatillos are
softened and slightly charred, about 7 minutes.

3. Let the vegetables cool to room
temperature. Transfer them to a blender with
the cilantro and puree until smooth. Season
with salt and pepper to taste. Store in an
airtight container in the refrigerator for up to
a week or freeze for up to 2 months.

SIMPLE WAYS TO USE IT

- Treat it like a better version of ketchup and eat it with anything that would benefit from a flavor bump—simple grilled pork chops or chicken breasts, fried fish or shrimp.

- Get jiggy with it and mix 1 part salsa with 2 parts soft butter, cover, stick it back in the fridge, then throw a pat of it on seared scallops.

- Love chicken soup? Well, love it even more when tomatillo salsa gives it some tang and heat.

- Add some chicken stock, and you have the world's greatest stewing liquid for chicken and pork.

- Tacos, baby. Like my *Tacos de Chivo* (page 139). Do I even have to mention that?

TOMATILLOS

The star of the show is the tomatillo, the most underrated fruit there is. I remember when I had to go searching the streets for these green guys encased in papery husks. Now you can find them at Whole Foods. Yet I've met so many people who still keep their distance, because nobody's told them how to prep the tomatillo. Allow me. It's easy: Peel off the husk and discard it. Touch the tomatillo—you feel that sticky stuff? Rinse it off under running water, rubbing the skin with your fingers as you do. Dry them and, boom, you're ready.

Storing Tomatillos
You can keep tomatillos in their husks in your vegetable drawer for up to three weeks.

Roasting Tomatillos
When tomatillos are raw, they're deliciously tart, but roasting them mellows their acidity and turns it tangy, almost sweet. Don't be afraid of the black char that develops as they cook—it's your friend and will provide, as my mom always says, a profoundness of flavor that is distinctly Mexican. When they're done, you'll notice that the little fruits have released a golden liquid. Do not leave this stuff in the pan! That's the stuff that makes the salsa addictive.

ROASTING THE REST

The tomatillo might be the handsome dude at the party, but that doesn't mean you should neglect his friends. So keep a close eye on the onion and garlic as they roast. They might be done before the tomatillos, so be ready to take them out of the broiler first—though, please, not until they're fully cooked and sweet.

SERRANO CHILES

It's worth looking around for these slim green chiles. They provide this grassy sharpness, along with prickly heat, that I love. But if you like your salsa a bit milder, feel free to substitute jalapeños.

CILANTRO

Notice that I wait until the salsa cools before blending in the cilantro. That's no accident. If you add it to the hot tomatillo mixture, you'd better say bye-bye to that bright green color and to that fresh cilantro flavor.

mini chorizo and potato tortas

One of my favorite taco combinations is also awesome crammed between bread. If the carb-on-carb pairing sounds funny to you, my best argument in its favor is one bite of this sandwich.

SERVES 4

2 medium Yukon Gold potatoes, peeled and quartered (about ½ pound)

Salt

1 tablespoon canola or vegetable oil

1 pound Mexican chorizo, casings removed, or Aarón's Chorizo (page 102)

Four 4-inch-long pambazos, teleras, or French bread rolls

⅛ small head red cabbage, very thinly sliced (about 1 cup)

1 tablespoon apple cider vinegar

2 tablespoons olive oil

½ cup crumbled queso fresco (preferably the Cacique brand) or lightly salty feta

1 pickled jalapeño, thinly sliced (yup, seeds too, if you can take the heat)

1 cup Roasted Tomatillo Salsa (page 78)

1. Cover the potatoes with cold water in a medium pot and salt well. Bring to a simmer over medium-high heat and cook the potatoes until they're tender and cooked through, 15 to 20 minutes. Drain the potatoes, let them cool until you can handle them, and cut them into small chunks.

2. Heat the canola oil in a large skillet over medium heat. Add the chorizo and cook, stirring and breaking it up with a spoon, until it's cooked through and slightly browned. Drain off some of the fat, add the chunks of potato, and gently mix them with the chorizo. Season with salt to taste.

3. Split the rolls lengthwise and remove and discard some of the soft insides. Toast the rolls until they're a light golden brown. Pile on the chorizo-potato mixture.

4. In a bowl, mix the cabbage with the vinegar and olive oil.

5. Divide the queso fresco, jalapeño slices, and cabbage among the sandwiches. Drizzle on a tablespoon or two of the Roasted Tomatillo Salsa and add the top of the roll. Serve right away with a bowl of the remaining salsa on the side, because you might want more.

sausage chili verde
with hominy and pumpkin

For a quick dinner on a cold night, nothing beats chili. But this one-pot meal isn't like all the others. Instead of beans, you have hearty hominy and chunks of winter squash. And instead of the same old tomatoey sauce, you have an eye-catching, super-tangy green one made from tomatillos.

SERVES 4

2 tablespoons extra virgin olive oil

1 large yellow onion, coarsely chopped

1 pound sausage meat, mild or hot

1½ teaspoons dried whole oregano (preferably Mexican), crumbled

3 large garlic cloves, very finely chopped

2 cups Roasted Tomatillo Salsa (page 78)

One 15-ounce can hominy

½ cup chopped fresh cilantro

½ pound peeled, seeded sugar pumpkin or butternut squash, cut into ½-inch cubes (about 2 cups)

Salt (optional)

1. Heat the olive oil in a Dutch oven or large saucepan over medium heat. Add the onion and cook, stirring occasionally, until just translucent, about 4 minutes.

2. Add the sausage meat and cook, stirring and breaking it up, until it's browned, about 10 minutes.

3. Spoon out and discard the excess fat, leaving 1 to 2 tablespoons in the pan. Stir in the oregano and garlic and cook, stirring, for about 3 minutes more.

4. Stir in the Roasted Tomatillo Salsa, the hominy along with all of its liquid, the cilantro, and the pumpkin. Bring to a boil, reduce the heat to medium-low, and simmer, covered, until the pumpkin cubes are tender, 15 to 20 minutes.

5. Taste and season with salt, if necessary. Serve right away.

pork ribs braised in tomatillo salsa

Tomatillos and pork go together like cheese and burgers. The tangy acidity cuts through pork's richness and makes each bite of tender meat more exciting than the next. Beans make it a one-pot meal.

SERVES 4

2 pounds pork spareribs, cut into individual ribs

Salt and freshly ground black pepper

2 tablespoons vegetable oil

2 cups Roasted Tomatillo Salsa (page 78)

3 cups unsalted chicken stock (low-sodium store-bought is fine)

2 cups drained Great Northern or other white beans (cooked yourself or rinsed canned)

½ cup chopped fresh cilantro

1. Generously season the ribs with salt and pepper. Heat the oil in a large pot over high heat. Brown the ribs in the oil on all sides, in batches if necessary. As they finish browning, transfer them to a plate.

2. Reduce the heat to medium, pour the Roasted Tomatillo Salsa into the pot, and cook, stirring often and scraping the bottom of the pan with a wooden spoon to get at all those browned pork bits, about 5 minutes. Add the stock, bring to a simmer, and then add back all the pork ribs. Adjust the heat so that the liquid simmers gently. Cook, covered, until the ribs are very tender, 2 to 2½ hours.

3. Add the beans and simmer, uncovered, until they're heated through, about 10 minutes. Stir in the cilantro and serve right away.

chilaquiles

Mexican cooks don't waste a thing. When their tortillas get stale, they fry them to make chips, then soak those chips in sauce so they're simultaneously soft *and* crunchy. The resulting masterpiece is called *chilaquiles*, and though it's traditionally eaten in the morning, I've been known to whip it up for friends at all hours. This particular recipe is a riff on the version my mom served at her restaurant, Zarela—a sort of casserole of tortilla strips, chicken, and bubbly cheese that's sauced with easy and amazing Roasted Tomatillo Salsa at the very last minute. I can't imagine a better party dish.

SERVES 4

12 corn tortillas

2 cups vegetable oil, for frying

1 pound Monterey Jack cheese, shredded (about 4 cups)

3 cups shredded cooked chicken

2 cups crème fraîche or sour cream

3 cups Roasted Tomatillo Salsa (page 78)

½ cup heavy cream

1. Line a baking sheet with a few layers of paper towels.

2. Cut the tortillas in half. A few at a time, stack the halved tortillas and cut them into ¼-inch-wide strips. Heat the oil in a deep heavy saucepan (you can also use a deep-fryer) over medium heat to 350°F or until it's hot enough so that a test tortilla strip bubbles and sizzles when you drop it into the oil. Fry the tortilla strips in batches, a large handful at a time (but no more), removing each batch with a skimmer as soon as the strips are crisp and have stopped sizzling. Drain them on the paper towels and let them cool to room temperature.

3. While the tortilla strips are cooling, preheat the oven to 350°F.

4. Combine the tortilla strips, cheese, and chicken in a large bowl; toss to distribute the ingredients evenly. Place the mixture in a wide, shallow ovenproof pan (a 13 by 9-inch baking dish is perfect). Spread the crème fraîche over the top and bake until the mixture is heated through, about 25 minutes.

5. Meanwhile, heat the Roasted Tomatillo Salsa in a small saucepan over medium-low heat just until it simmers. Stir in the cream and cook for another minute, stirring often to keep it from scorching. Pour the sauce over the *chilaquiles* and serve right away.

tamarind-pasilla paste

Some kids grow up eating chocolate bars and Skittles. But I grew up south of the border, sucking on tamarind candies coated in sugar and chile powder. That sweet-tart flavor followed by a gentle, welcome burn is Mexico in a bite. It's one of the fundamental flavor profiles—like the primary colors of cuisine—that I look to when I'm dreaming up dishes.

It's always on my mind as I shop. When I'm at the market and come across a beautiful duck breast or lamb chop—anything, really, so long as it's nice and fatty—I start thinking how I can sic the sticky pulp from the tamarind pod on this bad boy, because I know it'll cut right through the meat's richness, like a samurai sword through a wheel of queso fresco. Finally, I figured I'd make it easy on myself and come up with a formula for a dose of tamarind that would always hit the spot.

If you've been paying attention so far, you might be able to guess the base for this versatile puree. Yup, charred vegetables, like tomato and onion, that provide the stage on which the tamarind can shine. I turn to the pasilla chile to deliver a little heat, which you know you love, because its spiciness comes with a little sweetness, too, that reminds me of the star of the show.

tamarind-pasilla paste

MAKES 3 CUPS

3 tablespoons olive oil

4 pasilla chiles, stemmed, seeded, and deveined

1 large white onion, quartered

10 whole garlic cloves, peeled

4 plum tomatoes, cored and halved lengthwise

Salt and freshly ground black pepper

1½ cups strained tamarind pulp (see page 89)

1. Bring 1 cup water to a boil in a small saucepan. Line a plate with paper towels.

2. Heat 2 tablespoons of the olive oil in a medium skillet over medium-high heat until it begins to dance. Add the pasillas and fry on both sides until they're puffed up, about 15 seconds total. Transfer the chiles to the paper towels to drain. Put them in a small bowl, pour in the boiling water, and let them soak until they're soft, about 15 minutes. Drain the chiles and reserve them and the soaking liquid separately.

3. Discard the oil and wipe the skillet clean. Set it back over medium-high heat. In a large bowl, toss the onion, garlic, and tomatoes with the remaining 1 tablespoon oil. Season with salt and pepper, toss gently, and put them in the hot skillet. Cook about 7 minutes on each side, until they're charred, with visible black spots. Transfer the vegetables to a clean bowl and let them cool to room temperature.

4. Put the tamarind pulp, chiles, ½ cup of the soaking liquid, and the roasted vegetables in a blender or food processor and blend until smooth.

5. Store it in an airtight container in the refrigerator for up to a week or in the freezer for up to a month.

SIMPLE WAYS TO USE IT

- To soup up your favorite soup, mix tamarind puree into your stock until it tastes awesome. Whether it's chicken noodle or vegetable, try topping it with some fried tortilla strips at the last minute to add a little crunch.

- Stir in some brown sugar and an Asian hot sauce, and you have a killer dip for grilled shrimp or chicken skewers.

- Lime juice and olive oil turn this paste into a vibrant dressing that moonlights as a sauce if you spoon a little over a piece of fish.

TAMARIND

You'd never guess from its mild-mannered appearance—a brown pod that sort of looks like a cross between a string bean and a "shell-on" peanut—that it's one of the tastiest fruits out there. It's one of those ingredients that bring so much natural flavor and complexity that you hardly have to lift a finger to turn it into something tasty. So it breaks my heart that cooks seem so daunted by it. Fortunately, it's super easy to use and you can buy it in two forms.

Fresh Pods

Once you peel off the pale brown pods, you'll see dark, glistening flesh clinging to big seeds, with some stringy fibers on the outside. That's nature's candy right there. You can roll the flesh in sugar and maybe some chile powder and you've got a great party snack. To get at the flesh, pull off and discard those strings. Put the tamarind in a bowl and add warm water just to cover. Let it soak for 15 minutes, rubbing it now and then with your fingers to loosen the flesh from the seeds. Pour it through a sieve into another bowl, pushing the tamarind against the sieve so the flesh passes through, leaving the seeds and fibers behind. (You'll need 6 to 8 fresh pods to get 1½ cups pulp.)

Tamarind Paste

Sold in blocks in Asian and Indian grocery stores, tamarind paste is the pulp of the fruit that someone has kindly extracted from the pod just for you. To use it, chop it coarsely and add it to a saucepan with water, about 2 cups for every cup of paste. Simmer, occasionally smooshing the paste with a spoon, until you have a smooth liquid. Pour it through a sieve into a bowl, pressing the solids against the sieve and discarding the stuff that's left behind.

PASILLA CHILES

When slender fresh chilaca chiles are dried—maybe laid out on a blanket in the sun, as families did back in the day—they shrivel and darken as their flavor intensifies. When they're wrinkly and nearly black, they're called pasillas, which means "little raisins." You'll see why when you taste them. Along with some nice heat—powerful but not overwhelming—is the sort of sweetness that brings to mind dried fruit. You'll almost always have to seed and devein them before you cook with them.

Select pasillas that don't snap or crumble when you bend them—they're sold in bags, but feel free to fondle those puppies through the plastic—and that have no pale spots or broken bits. Store them in an airtight bag in a cool, dark place for up to six months.

Quick tip: Fry pasillas in a little oil until they're puffed and crispy, and you've got a badass garnish for salads, soups, or anything else that would benefit from a flavorful crunch.

tamarind-tomatillo lamb shanks

L amb shanks can make a statement: Everyone at the table gets their own big ol' bone bearing meat so tender that you could cut it off with a butter knife. Yet flavor is how you make the most lasting impression, so whether you keep the shanks intact or shred the meat, your guests will never forget these.

SERVES 4

3 or 4 dried avocado leaves (see Note)

4 lamb shanks (approximately 1 pound each)

Salt

2½ pounds fresh tomatillos

1 cup Tamarind-Pasilla Paste (page 88)

3 tablespoons extra virgin olive oil

2 bunches fresh cilantro, stems discarded and leaves chopped

3 garlic cloves, very finely chopped

12 corn tortillas, warmed, for serving

Julienned radish and finely chopped fresh cilantro, for garnish

1. Preheat the oven to 325°F.

2. Put the avocado leaves in a dry cast-iron skillet over medium-high heat and toast, turning them over frequently, until they're fragrant, 1 to 2 minutes. Put the leaves in a Dutch oven.

3. Lay the lamb shanks over the avocado leaves. Sprinkle the shanks generously with salt (about 2 teaspoons) and cover the pot. Put it in the oven. Roast the lamb until it's very tender and falling off the bone, 2½ to 3 hours.

4. While the lamb is roasting, husk and rinse the tomatillos and put them in a medium saucepan. Just cover them with cold water and bring to a boil. Reduce the heat and simmer until they're tender, 10 to 12 minutes.

5. Drain the tomatillos and transfer them to a food processor or blender. Add the Tamarind-Pasilla Paste, olive oil, cilantro, garlic, and 1 teaspoon salt. Puree until the mixture is smooth.

(continued)

6. When the lamb is fully cooked, transfer the shanks to a platter. Drain off and discard the fat left in the bottom of the Dutch oven and discard the avocado leaves.

7. Pour the tamarind-tomatillo puree into the Dutch oven and put it over medium-high heat on the stovetop. Cook, stirring frequently and scraping the bottom with a wooden spoon to dislodge the tasty browned bits from the bottom, until the sauce starts to thicken, 10 to 15 minutes.

8. Remove the meat from the bone or leave the shanks intact. Put the meat back in the pot and cook it for another 5 minutes or so, basting to bring the flavors together.

9. Serve the meat and sauce with the tortillas. Garnish with the radish and cilantro.

NOTE: If you can't find dried avocado leaves, you can get a vague approximation of their herbal, fennel-like flavor by roasting the lamb shanks with a few bay leaves and a sprinkle of slightly crushed anise or fennel seeds.

duck leg pozole

This isn't your typical pozole, the soupy stew packed with pork and hominy that I suck down on the streets and in the markets of Mexico, like a kid in the United States might do to his bowl of chicken noodle. Nope, this modern version has a sweet, tangy broth and some delicious duck mingling with that beautiful, starchy hominy. Don't forget the fixings! They add layers of awesome texture and flavors.

SERVES 4

¾ cup Tamarind-Pasilla Paste (page 88)

1 quart chicken stock (low-sodium store-bought is fine)

1 tablespoon honey

2 confit duck legs

Two 15-ounce cans white hominy, drained

garnish

Finely chopped white onion

Chopped fresh cilantro

Dried whole oregano (preferably Mexican), crumbled

Lime wedges

1. Stir together the Tamarind-Pasilla Paste, chicken stock, and honey in a large heavy saucepan over medium heat. Bring to a boil, reduce the heat, and simmer, uncovered, until the mixture has thickened slightly, 15 to 20 minutes.

2. While the broth simmers, remove and discard the skin and bones from the duck. Shred the meat.

3. Once the broth has thickened, add the hominy and shredded duck. Simmer, covered, for 10 minutes to bring the flavors together.

4. Serve big bowls of pozole with bowls of onion, cilantro, oregano, and lime wedges and let your guests garnish their own servings.

pan-seared duck breasts with tamarind sauce

This is for everybody who's ever ordered duck at a fancy restaurant and fallen head over Manolos for it. The meat is pink and tender, each slice wearing a little cap of crispy, crispy skin. On the plate is this velvety, tangy sauce that tastes like a hundred cooks must have chipped in to make it. But just when you think you could never make anything so sophisticated and pretty at home, here I come to show you that it's not so hard at all.

SERVES 4

2 tablespoons unsalted butter

2 medium carrots, finely chopped

1 large white or yellow onion, finely chopped

2 stalks celery, finely chopped

6 whole garlic cloves, peeled

1 cup canned crushed tomatoes

2 cups red wine or port

1 quart homemade duck stock or chicken stock (low-sodium store-bought is fine)

2 canela sticks (Mexican cinnamon; see page 104)

4 whole star anise

3 fresh or dried bay leaves

1 small bunch fresh thyme

½ cup Tamarind-Pasilla Paste (page 88)

4 duck breasts, about ¾ pound each

Salt and freshly ground black pepper

1. Melt the butter in a large Dutch oven over medium heat. Add the carrots, onion, celery, and garlic and cook, stirring occasionally, until they've softened and browned, about 10 minutes. Add the tomatoes and cook, stirring, for another 2 minutes. Pour in the red wine and bring it to a strong simmer, scraping the bottom of the pot with a wooden spoon. Let the wine bubble away until it has reduced by half.

2. Add the duck stock, canela, star anise, and bay leaves. Bring back to a strong simmer and cook until the sauce is reduced by two-thirds, about 30 minutes.

3. Stir in the thyme and the Tamarind-Pasilla Paste and simmer for 5 minutes. Strain the sauce through a fine-mesh sieve into a clean saucepan. Discard the solids.

4. Preheat the oven to 400°F. Cut apart the whole duck breasts. Prick the skin of the duck in numerous places with a sharp knife.

5. Heat over medium-low heat an ovenproof skillet large enough to hold the duck breasts in one layer with room to spare. Generously season the duck breasts with salt and pepper. Place them in the pan skin side down. Cook until the skin has begun to brown and a lot of the fat has rendered out, about 3 minutes. Drain off most of the fat and flip the duck skin side up. Put the pan in the oven and cook about 5 minutes, until the skin is brown and crispy and the duck registers 145°F on an instant-read thermometer. Let the duck rest on a cutting board for about 5 minutes.

6. Gently reheat the sauce if necessary. Spoon 2 tablespoons of sauce onto each plate. Slice the duck breasts crosswise on the bias and arrange the slices on top of the sauce. Serve right away.

roasted lamb with pomegranate-tamarind sauce

Leave it to lamb to stand up to this bold sauce, a syrupy, deep-dark liquid that you'll be tempted to eat by the spoonful. There's pomegranate juice in there, and the addition of the seeds at the end provides a bonus of exhilarating tartness and crunch.

SERVES 4

3 tablespoons sugar

1 cup pomegranate juice (such as Pom brand)

1¼ cups chicken stock (low-sodium store-bought is fine)

¼ cup Tamarind-Pasilla Paste (page 88)

One 1½- to 2-pound boneless lamb loin

1 tablespoon olive oil

Salt and freshly ground black pepper

Fresh pomegranate seeds (see page 13)

1. Combine the sugar, juice, stock, and Tamarind-Pasilla Paste in a heavy medium saucepan over medium heat. Cook and stir until the sugar dissolves, then increase the heat so the mixture simmers. Cook, stirring often, until the liquid has thickened and reduced to a little less than 1 cup, about 20 minutes. Turn the heat to very low and keep the sauce warm while you cook the lamb.

2. While the sauce is cooking, heat a large ovenproof skillet over medium-high heat. Drizzle the lamb with the olive oil, season generously with salt, and place in the pan. Cook on each side for 5 minutes, transfer to a cutting board, and let rest for 3 minutes. Cut the lamb crosswise into ½-inch-thick slices.

3. Put the slices on plates and spoon on the sauce. Sprinkle with the pomegranate seeds and serve right away.

aarón's chorizo

I have a tattoo on my right forearm that says "old school" in honor of my grandmother Aida Gabilondo. She was the first in my family's three generations of cookbook authors. She was the one who taught my mom to cook.

And, man, did she love chorizo, the red-tinted Mexican sausage that I'd put up against any other sausage in the world in a Most Delicious competition. When I was no taller than the kitchen counter, I'd watch her make her own and fastidiously pack identical little portions of it, which she'd store in the freezer in an empty Coca-Cola box. Anytime she felt the urge, she'd dip into this treasure chest and pull out the perfect amount of chorizo to accompany her morning eggs.

This is a sort of spin-off of my grandmother's recipe. And if you assumed you'd need meat grinders and sausage casings to make chorizo, think again. It's as easy as marinating ground meat overnight. Then you're ready to fry it in a pan until it's lightly browned and still juicy. In Mexico, you'll see salty, spicy bits of chorizo chilling with chunks of potato in tortillas when you order one of my favorite snacks, *tacos con chorizo y papas*. You'll see chorizo in sandwiches, stuffed into empanadas, and piled on top of thick tortilla-like fried dough called *sopes* (see page 60). But just about any recipe that calls for sausage would welcome chorizo, and you'll find yourself using it in ways you never imagined—because it tastes so damn good.

aarón's chorizo

1 pound ground beef chuck

1 pound ground pork

3 garlic cloves, very finely chopped

1 tablespoon salt

¼ cup white wine vinegar

1 teaspoon freshly ground black pepper

1 teaspoon ground canela (Mexican
    cinnamon; see page 104), or
    ½ teaspoon ground cinnamon

1 teaspoon ground star anise

½ teaspoon ground cloves

2 tablespoons crushed dried oregano
    (preferably Mexican)

¼ cup dry white wine

1 teaspoon sugar

½ cup ancho chile powder

1. Put the ground beef and pork in a large bowl. Add the garlic, salt, and vinegar and mix well (your hands are the best tools for this job). Sprinkle with the pepper, canela, star anise, cloves, and oregano and mix well. Add the wine and sugar and mix well.

2. Bring 1 cup water to a boil in a small saucepan. Put the chile powder in a small bowl, pour in the boiling water, and stir well to make a paste. Let it cool to room temperature. Work the paste into the meat with your fingers until it's well incorporated. Cover and refrigerate overnight before you use it. Store in 2-ounce portions in ziplock bags in the refrigerator for up to a week, or freeze for up to 3 months. (That's the perfect amount for 3 eggs!)

SIMPLE WAYS TO USE IT

- Your breakfast scrambled eggs will never be the same after you've had them with chorizo alongside instead of those mystery patties you get at diners.

- Those eggs and chorizo also form the foundation for breakfast burrito bliss, particularly if you add some beans, cheese, and a little guacamole or sour cream.

- Chorizo and potatoes are a culinary dream team, so next time you roast or boil potatoes, chop them into chunks and finish them in a pan of just-cooked chorizo.

- Warm tortillas, chorizo, chopped white onion, cilantro, and a squeeze of lime are all you need for tremendous tacos. If you spoon on Roasted Tomatillo Salsa (page 78), all the better.

NO, NOT *THAT* CHORIZO

Don't confuse Mexican chorizo with the Spanish sausage of the same name. The Mexican version, besides being spiced differently, is a raw product that you must cook to an awesome state of juicy deliciousness, while the Spanish kind is cured and ready to eat in chewy slices. It's kind of like the difference between Italian sweet sausage links and salami. Each different, both great.

GRINDIN'!

When you're buying ground meat for this recipe, here are some things to keep in mind. Meat that's been overground produces sausage that's too dense no matter what you do to it. So, ideally, you'd grind your own meat (perhaps with the grinder attachment for your KitchenAid mixer) or get meat that's been ground to order. The guys at the butcher counter will do this for you, especially if you ask nice. Or you can look in the meat case for already ground meat that looks like loose little squiggles of meat rather than paste.

Once you've found great ground meat, treat it gently. You want to mix the pork and beef together with the spices just until it's all nicely combined. Resist the temptation to overmix—you'll know you've gone too far when the meat starts sticking to your hands.

CANELA

If you haven't tasted canela, then you've probably never had real cinnamon. No, seriously, the stuff called cinnamon that you put in your apple pies is actually cassia. It has an astringent, assertive flavor compared to canela (also called true cinnamon or Ceylon cinnamon), which smells unbelievably sweet and fragrant. Canela is pretty easy to find—Latin grocery stores almost always have it, and so do some supermarkets. It typically comes in sticks, not ground, so you'll have to grind about two in a spice grinder to get the 1 teaspoonful you need for this recipe. If you must (come on, try canela at least once!), use half a teaspoon of regular ground cinnamon.

ANCHO CHILE POWDER

Because Mexican flavors have been blowing up in the United States for years, it's now pretty easy to find the ancho chile powder I call for in this recipe. Even so, making your own is simple and ensures that the ground chiles will be full of flavor: Preheat your oven to 400°F. Remove the seeds and stems from 2 ounces ancho chiles. Put the chiles on a baking sheet and toast them in the hot oven until they start to smell really good, about 2 minutes. Then grind them to a powder in a spice grinder or blender.

ALL RIGHT, ALL RIGHT

Now, you know I want you to make your own chorizo to see how easy and tasty it can be. But if you're dying to make my Chorizo and Potato Empanadas (page 110) or Chorizo and Corn Bread Stuffing (page 109) and don't have the time or energy to mix some stuff in a bowl and marinate it, well, fine. You can buy some at the store. I won't be mad at you.

baked clams with chorizo

Chorizo is one of those fantastically flavorful foods that instantly improve whatever they touch. Once you brown it in a pan with a little tomato and onion, your work for this dish is just about done. The mixture makes a killer topping for briny beauties that you cook just until they're tender and the bread crumbs sprinkled on top are brown and crispy.

If you have your fish store open the clams for you, rush them home and cook 'em as soon as you can.

SERVES 4 AS AN APPETIZER

¼ cup Aarón's Chorizo (page 102)

½ medium white onion, finely chopped

1 medium tomato, seeded and chopped

¼ cup tomato sauce

2 teaspoons spicy mustard, such as Creole mustard

12 medium clams, such as littlenecks, on the half shell

½ cup coarse fresh bread crumbs

1. Preheat the oven to 400°F.

2. Heat a medium skillet over medium-high heat. Fry the chorizo, onion, and tomato, breaking up the chorizo as it cooks, until it begins to brown. Stir in the tomato sauce and mustard and cook for 5 minutes more.

3. Set the clams on a baking sheet. Top each one with some of the chorizo mixture, and top that with some of the bread crumbs. Bake the clams until the bread crumbs are golden brown, about 8 minutes. Serve right away.

black beans with chorizo and chipotle crema

Just because beans are served on the side doesn't mean they should be an afterthought. Where I come from, cooks are just as proud of their beans as they are of their moles. And my version is anything but bland, thanks to my chorizo and smoky chipotle-spiked cream.

SERVES 6

One 16-ounce package dried black beans (about 2 cups)

2 yellow onions (1 small, skin on and halved; 1 large, chopped)

2 sprigs fresh epazote, 1 teaspoon dried epazote, or 2 bay leaves

2 tablespoons olive oil

1 generous cup Aarón's Chorizo (page 102)

4 garlic cloves, very finely chopped

Salt

1 cup crema fresca (preferably the Cacique brand), or a scant cup full-fat sour cream thinned with 2 tablespoons buttermilk

2 to 3 tablespoons Garlic-Chipotle Love (page 6)

Finely chopped fresh cilantro and thinly sliced scallion greens, for garnish

1. Rinse and drain the beans, then pick them over to remove any stones. Put the beans in a large heavy pot, such as a Dutch oven, and add enough cold water to cover them by 2 inches. Add the onion halves and the epazote or bay leaves. Bring to a boil, reduce the heat, and simmer the beans, uncovered, until the beans are tender and creamy but the skins have not burst, 1½ to 2 hours. Discard the onion halves and the epazote sprigs or bay leaves.

CANNED BEAN VARIATION

I tell everyone I can how easy and inexpensive it is to start with dried beans instead of buying them already cooked in cans. But I understand that you don't always have time to soak and simmer. And you know what? Canned beans can be pretty damn tasty. Just substitute drained and rinsed black beans from three 15-ounce cans, leave out the halved onion, skip the first step, and add water instead of the reserved cooking liquid.

2. Heat the olive oil in a large, deep skillet over medium-high heat. Add the chopped onion and cook until it's lightly browned and tender, about 5 minutes. Add the chorizo and garlic and cook, breaking up the chorizo with a spoon and stirring occasionally, until it's browned, about 5 minutes. Spoon off and discard any visible grease.

3. Use a slotted spoon to transfer the beans to the skillet, reserving the cooking liquid. Add ½ cup of the cooking liquid and simmer gently for 5 minutes to let the flavors blend. If the beans look dry, gradually add more of the bean cooking liquid. Season with salt to taste.

4. Stir together the crema fresca and Garlic-Chipotle Love in a small bowl and serve over the beans. Garnish with chopped cilantro and sliced scallions.

chorizo and corn bread stuffing

I have a theory about why Thanksgiving is such a popular holiday. No, it's not the time you get off from work or hanging out with your weird uncle—it's the stuffing. Crispy, crunchy, mushy, chewy, the combination of textures is amazing and so is the flavor. But nothing compares to the pairing of sweet corn bread and spicy, salty chorizo. And be real; cilantro kicks parsley's butt any day.

MAKES 3 CUPS

1 pound Aarón's Chorizo (page 102)

1 medium white onion, finely chopped

1 medium carrot, finely chopped

1 celery stalk, finely chopped

3 garlic cloves, finely chopped

2 cups coarsely crumbled corn bread

¼ cup chopped fresh cilantro

½ cup chicken stock (low-sodium store-bought is fine)

1 tablespoon unsalted butter

Chopped fresh cilantro and grated cotija (preferably the Cacique brand), for garnish

1. Preheat the oven to 350°F.

2. Heat a large skillet over medium heat. Cook the chorizo, breaking it up with a spoon and stirring occasionally as it cooks, until it begins to brown, about 5 minutes. Add the onion, carrot, celery, and garlic and cook, stirring occasionally, until the vegetables have browned, about 10 minutes. Add the corn bread and cilantro. Gradually stir in enough of the stock so that the stuffing is not too dry but at the same time not too wet. Stir gently and well.

3. Butter a small casserole. Spread the stuffing in an even layer. Bake until it's heated through and lightly browned on top, about 20 minutes. Serve right away, garnished with the cilantro and cotija.

chorizo and potato empanadas

Just a little mixing and you've got awesome empanada dough that turns just about any filling into party food. In this case, I've got you covered with a sweet and salty mixture of potatoes and chorizo. Serve them hot from the oven with a bowl of salsa for dipping.

MAKES 10 EMPANADAS

dough

¾ cup all-purpose flour, plus more for kneading

½ cup masa harina (corn tortilla flour; see Resources, page 185)

½ teaspoon baking powder

½ teaspoon salt

¼ cup vegetable oil

½ cup warm water

filling

1 large boiling potato, peeled and cut into ½-inch cubes

1 generous cup Aarón's Chorizo (page 102)

1 small yellow onion, chopped

3 tablespoons sliced pimento-stuffed green olives

3 tablespoons golden raisins

1 teaspoon dried whole oregano (preferably Mexican)

Salt and freshly ground black pepper

1 egg beaten with 1 tablespoon water

Roasted Tomato–Chile de Árbol Salsa (page 52), for serving

1. To make the dough, stir together the flour, masa harina, baking powder, and salt in a large bowl. Stir in the oil and water and mix well. Turn out onto a floured surface and knead lightly to form a smooth, supple dough. (If you need more water, add it a teaspoon at a time to avoid making the dough sticky.) Wrap the dough in plastic wrap and chill it in the refrigerator for 20 minutes while you make the filling.

2. Put the potato in lightly salted water in a small saucepan, bring to a boil, and cook until tender, 5 to 7 minutes. Drain.

3. Meanwhile, in a heavy skillet over medium heat, cook the chorizo, stirring and breaking it up, for about 5 minutes. Add the onion and cook for another 5 minutes, until the onion is tender and translucent. Stir in the potato, olives, raisins, and oregano. Cook, stirring occasionally, until the mixture is heated through, 3 to 4 minutes. Season to taste with salt and pepper.

4. Preheat the oven to 375°F and lightly grease a large baking sheet.

5. Divide the dough into 10 balls. On a lightly floured surface, roll each ball out into a circle about 4 inches across. Place a couple of tablespoons of the filling just off-center on one circle, and fold the dough over to make a half circle. Crimp the edges with a fork to seal, and transfer the empanada to a baking sheet. Repeat with the remaining dough and filling.

6. Brush each empanada lightly with the egg. Use the tip of a paring knife to slash a few holes in the top of each empanada.

Bake until the empanadas are golden brown, about 25 minutes. Alternatively, you can fry the empanadas. Heat an inch or so of vegetable oil to 350°F in a large skillet. Fry the empanadas in batches of three, carefully flipping them over once, until they're golden brown and crispy, about 5 minutes. Transfer them to paper towels to drain, and let the oil return to 350°F before frying the next batch.

7. Serve warm with the Roasted Tomato–Chile de Árbol Salsa.

aarón's achiote paste

The Yucatán is like no other place in Mexico. When you're roaming the markets, you're almost as likely to bump into orbs of Dutch cheese as you are piles of habaneros. The funky mix of cultures and ingredients—Mayan, Spanish, Dutch—is fascinating stuff. But I bet you that any profound thoughts about colonialism or fifteenth-century trade routes disappear as soon as you spot a steaming heap of *cochinita pibil*.

It's my nominee for dish of the millennium: pork wrapped in banana leaf and cooked for hours in the oven—or in the traditional manner, in an outdoor pit. The result is so ridiculously tender and juicy that before you know it, you're back at the counter of the market stall, as if in a trance, ordering another kilo. Now you understand why I want to move to the Yucatán when I retire.

Ah, but there's more: Before it's cooked, the meat gets rubbed with a paste that includes a combination of ingredients—garlic, citrus, annatto seeds (more about those in a minute)—so remarkable that I made it the focus of this chapter. Making my version of this marinade is as simple as pressing the blend button. The paste packs big flavor and also imparts this wonderful copper color to whatever it touches. Once you have it on hand, almost any protein, from pork and chicken to lobster, shrimp, and meaty fish like swordfish and mahimahi, is fair game.

aarón's achiote paste

MAKE 1½ CUPS

2 large garlic cloves, roughly chopped

½ teaspoon ground cumin

2 teaspoons dried whole oregano
(preferably Mexican) or dried
marjoram

2 tablespoons achiote paste (see page 115
and Resources, page 185)

¼ cup olive oil

½ cup freshly squeezed lime juice

½ cup freshly squeezed orange juice

Combine all the ingredients in a blender.
Puree until the mixture is the consistency
of a smooth vinaigrette. Store in an airtight
container in the refrigerator for up to 2 weeks.

SIMPLE WAY TO USE IT

- The achiote paste makes a killer marinade, but sometimes you don't have time to let it do its thing. That's cool; you can always make it into a sauce by adding a cup or so of stock or water for every two tablespoons of paste. Simmer it over medium-low heat for 20 minutes, add some salt to taste, and you're golden.

ANNATTO (AKA ACHIOTE) SEEDS

I know what you're thinking: What the heck is an annatto seed? Well, it comes from a tropical plant that has these awesome-looking pods (imagine if bright-red porcupines grew on trees) that contain the seeds. And although it sounds exotic, it's really easy to find, partly because the seeds are used all over the world as natural dyes and partly because the odds are that wherever you live, there are some Mexicans, Cubans, or Puerto Ricans nearby who would break down in tears if they couldn't buy them at the store.

The seeds are one of those ingredients—tomatillos are another—that taste pretty mild by themselves, but with just a few partners, they transform into something amazing. They have a flinty, earthy flavor that's really easygoing.

In this recipe, you're not just using plain annatto seeds. Rather, you want to get your hands on annatto paste, the seeds blended with some spices and tomatoes. Cooks from the Yucatán use pastes like this (they're known as *recados*) all the time. The El Yucateco brand is sold just about everywhere and hits the spot.

RAW GARLIC

. . . is not my thing. So do me a favor and don't eat this paste raw. Between the garlic and annatto, it's at its best when it's cooked.

SOUR ORANGES

I can really get down with the "If it grows together, it goes together" theory of cooking. A prime example is the explosion of deliciousness you get when annatto seeds meet sour oranges, another of the most distinctive ingredients grown in the Yucatán. Known in Spanish as *naranjas agrias*, this citrus has a sharply sour, slightly bitter flavor that adds an incredible brightness to this marinade and helps tenderize whatever it hangs out with for a while. If you go to a fancy market, you might be able to find the sour orange called Seville, which would work well, or you can improvise, like I often do, and substitute a mixture of one part regular orange juice and one part lime juice—both freshly squeezed, please.

SALT

Where's the salt in this recipe? you wonder. Good question. There is none. Over time, salt draws out moisture from meat, and that's not what I want in a marinade. Instead, season your protein right before you cook it.

whole striped bass
with achiote and peppers

Nothing beats a whole fish for dramatic presentation, but it's also surprisingly easy to make. Have your fish store do the prep on it for you. Hit it with a quick marinade, then stuff some tasty veggies inside. Whether you cook it on the grill or in the oven, you'll have some serious beachfront Mexican flavor.

SERVES 2

One 3- to 4-pound whole branzino or wild striped bass, scaled and gutted

½ cup Aarón's Achiote Paste (page 114)

Salt and freshly ground black pepper

1 medium red bell pepper, stemmed, seeded, and very thinly sliced

1 medium yellow bell pepper, stemmed, seeded, and very thinly sliced

1 medium yellow or Spanish onion, thinly sliced

1 jalapeño or ½ serrano chile, thinly sliced (yup, seeds too, if you can take the heat)

2 medium tomatoes, cored and cut into large chunks

½ cup olive oil

2 banana leaves, fresh or thawed frozen (see Note, page 121)

Warm corn tortillas, for serving

1. Score the fish on both sides and rub the achiote paste all over. Season with salt and pepper and set the fish aside to rest for 20 minutes on the countertop.

2. In a large bowl, combine the bell peppers, onion, jalapeño, tomatoes, and olive oil. Season generously with salt and pepper. Stuff it inside the cavity of the fish. (It's okay if the cavity gapes open.)

3. Heat a grill to medium.

4. Lay 1 banana leaf on the grill, put the fish on it, and put the other banana leaf on top of the fish. Cook, covered, for 25 minutes, carefully turning it over once halfway through.

5. Place the fish on a large serving platter with spoons so diners can flake off some fish and mound it on warm tortillas with some of the stuffing.

NOTE: For oven cooking, preheat the oven to 425°F. Lay a banana leaf on a baking sheet, put the fish on it, and top with another banana leaf. Roast until the fish is just cooked through, about 30 minutes, and serve as above.

achiote-marinated stuffed baby chicken

When you pull these little birds from your oven, don't be surprised to see that their crispy skin is a stunning reddish-copper. That's from the achiote marinade, which also provides an awesome flavor boost. Between that and the tasty stuffing—salty chorizo, slightly sharp mustard greens, hearty potato—your dinner is guaranteed to be slammin'.

SERVES 4

2 poussins (baby chickens, about 1½ pounds each)

1 cup Aarón's Achiote Paste (page 114)

1 medium russet potato, peeled

Salt

2 large links (½ pound) Spanish chorizo (see page 103), diced

1 large yellow or Spanish onion, finely chopped

3 garlic cloves, chopped

1 bunch mustard greens, tough stems removed and leaves coarsely chopped

½ cup chicken stock (low-sodium store-bought is fine)

2 tablespoons sliced pitted green olives

Salt and freshly ground black pepper

1. The night before you plan to cook, rub the chickens all over with the achiote paste (underneath the skin, on the skin, inside the cavities). Let them marinate, covered, overnight in the refrigerator.

2. Cover the potato with cold water in a small saucepan and add a good amount of salt. Bring to a simmer over medium-high heat and cook until the potato is tender and cooked through, about 25 minutes. Drain the potato, and when it's cool enough to handle, cut it into small chunks.

3. Heat a large skillet over medium heat. Drop in the chorizo and cook, stirring occasionally, until it's crispy, about 5 minutes. Add the onion and garlic and cook, stirring occasionally, for another 2 minutes. Add the mustard greens and chicken stock and cook, stirring and scraping the bottom of the pan

with a wooden spoon to get at the tasty stuff that's stuck to the pan, for about 2 minutes or just until all the greens have wilted. Stir in the potatoes and olives. Season to taste with salt and pepper. Remove the pan from the heat and let the stuffing cool to room temperature.

4. While the stuffing is cooling, preheat the oven to 375°F. Remove the chickens from the refrigerator.

5. Divide the stuffing equally and spoon into the cavity of each bird. Arrange the birds with plenty of space between them on a rack on a baking sheet or in a roasting pan. Roast the chickens until an instant-read thermometer inserted into the thickest part of the thigh reads 180°F, about 40 minutes.

yucatán-style pork, my way

Here it is, my version of the Yucatán's finest porky achievement, the stunning orange-hued, spoon-tender *cochinita pibil*. There's no limit to the ways to celebrate its greatness—a mound of it beside beans and rice, a heap on top of tostadas, a tangle inside tortillas for tacos or a nice, crusty roll for a torta.

SERVES 6

6 pounds boneless pork shoulder (not lean), cut into 3-inch chunks

2 teaspoons salt

1 teaspoon freshly ground black pepper

½ cup Aarón's Achiote Paste (page 114)

1 large white onion, halved and sliced

3 banana leaves, fresh or thawed frozen (see Note)

Pickled Onions, My Way (page 150), for garnish (optional)

Warm corn tortillas, for serving

1. Put the pork in a large bowl and rub with the salt and pepper. Rub the pork with the achiote paste to coat well. Add the onion and stir well to combine. Set aside.

2. To prepare the banana leaves, wipe off any white residue with a damp paper towel and use kitchen shears to trim off any brown edges. Toast the banana leaves by holding them over a high flame on a gas stove. Working with 1 leaf at a time, grab the leaf at both ends and move it slowly over the flame until it becomes flexible and slightly shiny but not charred, about 20 seconds per side. (If you don't have a gas stove, simmer the leaves for 10 minutes in a large pot of hot water. Drain and proceed when the leaves are cool enough to handle.)

3. Line a roasting pan with the leaves, overlapping them to make a smooth base. Pour the achiote-rubbed pork and sliced onion into the pan and fold the banana leaves over the top to seal, tucking in the excess around the sides. Seal the top of the pan with foil and refrigerate for at least 5 hours or overnight.

4. When you're ready to roast, remove the pan from the refrigerator and let it sit for about an hour, or until the meat comes to room temperature. Preheat the oven to 400°F.

5. Put the covered pan in the oven and roast until the pork is very tender, about 2½ hours.

6. To serve, remove the foil and fold back the banana leaves. Garnish with Pickled Onions, My Way, if desired. Bring the roasting pan to the table and spoon the pork into warm corn tortillas.

NOTE: Banana leaves impart an awesomely herbal flavor to the pork, but they should not be eaten. They are readily available frozen in Asian markets and in many grocery stores. If you can't find banana leaves, no problem: Line the roasting pan with overlapping layers of heavy-duty foil and fold the edges over the top to seal.

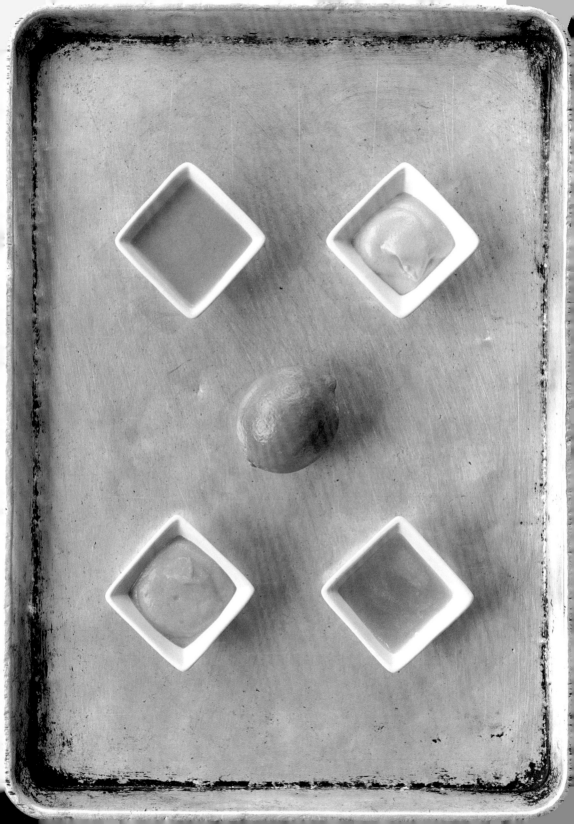

mango–aji
amarillo puree

Sometimes I wonder if when I was little, my mom gave me a chipotle to suck on instead of a pacifier. Because I grew up to be a chile fiend. And just when I thought Mexico's endless variety—dried and fresh, spicy and mild, green and red, orange and blackish— was all I'd ever need, I found a new obsession. I was working for Douglas Rodriguez, a genius with Latin flavors of all kinds, and he introduced me to the pleasures of Peruvian food, which has become one of my favorite South American cuisines. Peru is where potatoes come from. It's probably the birthplace of ceviche. Its food is influenced by Japanese, Chinese, and Indian immigrants. And it's responsible for the amazing chile called aji amarillo. Sold as a paste, this citrusy, mildly spicy product is right up there with chipotles in adobo as one of the most delicious things you can find in a can or jar.

I've used the paste in so many ways in my kitchen, but this is the one I keep coming back to. One day, the bright yellow color of the chile paste got my mind thinking of other brightly colored ingredients like sweet, juicy mango. Another lightbulb went off when I noticed how much the paste resembled yellow mustard, so I started experimenting, adding a little Dijon for some vinegary bite. When this trio teams up, you get an addictive fusion of flavors that you won't soon forget.

mango–aji amarillo puree

MAKES 1¼ CUPS

1 cup mango puree (see page 125)

2 tablespoons Dijon mustard

2 tablespoons aji amarillo paste (preferably
the Doña Isabel brand)

1 teaspoon agave nectar or honey

Grated zest of 1 lime

1 tablespoon freshly squeezed lime juice

Put all the ingredients in a bowl and whisk well
until the mixture is smooth. Store in an airtight
container in the refrigerator for up to a week.

SIMPLE WAYS TO USE IT

- Turn a spoonful into dreamy mango vinaigrette by whisking in olive oil and some extra lime juice. I've used this to dress simple grilled chicken salad and even grilled watermelon.

- Brush it on shrimp or fish a few minutes before it's cooked through, and you're looking good.

- Add chunks of ripe mango, and you've got a perfect chip dip.

AJI AMARILLO PASTE

In Mexico, we call any spicy pepper a "chile," a word every American knows well. Yet in the rest of Latin America, they use the word "aji." The particular aji of my dreams is called aji amarillo (yellow chile), aka aji marisol (sunflower chile), though when it's fresh, it's actually bright orange. My favorite brand is Doña Isabel (available from Kalustyan's; see Resources, page 185). It's a godsend to sensitive souls who want to experience the wonderful fruity flavor of habaneros but don't feel like mapping out routes to the hospital to treat tongue burns. Aji amarillo has a lovely heat that doesn't explode onto your tongue, but rather slowly builds to a pleasant heat, like sitting in a field on a summer day.

MANGO PUREE

What a world we live in! There are so many sweet, delicious mangoes out there that no one can eat them all. So they don't go to waste, kind souls turn them into puree, which is sold fresh and frozen just about everywhere and is one of the stars of this sauce. Look for a puree that's got nothing in it but mangoes, or make your own by blending overripe mangoes with a little water and freezing it by the cupful in freezer bags.

YOUR DINNER, YOUR DECISION

Hitting just the right note of sweet and sour really makes this sauce sing. But remember, finding that final balance is up to you. Follow the recipe, and have a taste. Maybe the mango isn't as sweet as usual—that's cool, add a touch more honey. Perhaps it's a little too sweet—no prob, add another squeeze of lime.

LIME ZEST

The skin of citrus fruit is packed with aromatic oils that add a fragrant lift to whatever they touch. The key is shaving off just the thin skin and none of the bitter white pith. This can be tough with box graters, which aren't delicate enough for the task. So save those for cheese and get your hands on a Microplane zester. Its incredibly fine blades are perfect for the job.

tangerine and jicama slaw with chicharrón

Say bye-bye to the same old slaw. This one is all about different textures and flavors—soft, sweet-tart tangerine and crunchy peanuts mingling with crisp sticks of jicama and crackly pork rinds. The mango-aji dressing pulls it all together and makes sure every bite is a thrill.

SERVES 4 TO 6

6 large tangerines, mandarins, or tangelos

1 medium jicama, peeled and sliced into 2-inch-long matchsticks

2 cups very thinly sliced red cabbage (from about ¼ small head)

½ medium red onion, thinly sliced

½ cup Mango–Aji Amarillo Puree (page 124)

Juice of 1 lime

2 tablespoons extra virgin olive oil

1 teaspoon kosher salt

Freshly ground black pepper

1 cup crumbled pork rinds (*chicharrón*)

½ cup salted roasted peanuts, coarsely chopped

Finely chopped fresh cilantro and chives, for garnish

1. Peel the tangerines, separate them into segments, and place them in a large bowl. Add the jicama, cabbage, and onion and toss it all together.

2. Whisk the Mango–Aji Amarillo Puree, lime juice, olive oil, salt, and several generous grinds of black pepper in a small bowl. Pour the dressing over the slaw and toss gently to combine.

3. If you're not serving it right away, cover the bowl tightly with plastic wrap and keep it in the refrigerator for up to 4 hours.

4. Right before serving, sprinkle the slaw with the crumbled pork rinds and peanuts, toss just to combine, garnish with chopped cilantro and chives, and serve at once.

lobster ceviche with passion fruit

This is what my Mango–Aji Amarillo Puree was born to do. It adds an amazing depth of flavor and a little lip-tingling heat to big chunks of sweet lobster (or shrimp, if you don't feel like splurging) tossed with fruit juice, red onion, and other tasty stuff, turning a pleasant seafood salad into a life-altering ceviche.

SERVES 4

2 oranges

2 passion fruits

Two 1½-pound lobsters, cooked, chilled, and shelled

1 medium red onion, very thinly sliced

2 medium tomatoes, seeded and diced

2 scallions, thinly sliced

1 cup mango nectar

1 cup freshly squeezed orange juice

2 tablespoons freshly squeezed lime juice

½ cup Mango–Aji Amarillo Puree (page 124)

Finely chopped fresh cilantro

Salt and freshly ground black pepper

1 mango, peeled, seeded, and thinly sliced

1. Slice the rind and pith off the oranges. Use a sharp paring knife to slice the orange segments clean away from the membrane, dropping the segments into a large bowl and turning over the membranes like the pages of a book until all the segments have been trimmed free. Squeeze any remaining juice in the membrane into the bowl.

2. Cut the passion fruits in half. Use a spoon to scoop out the pulp from each half and press it through a coarse sieve to remove the seeds. Discard the seeds and add the juice and pulp to the bowl.

3. Cut the lobster meat into large bite-size pieces and put them in a large bowl. Add the onion, tomatoes, and scallions.

4. In a separate bowl, combine the mango nectar, orange juice, lime juice, and the Mango–Aji Amarillo Puree and stir well. Add the juice mixture to the lobster mixture, toss well, and season with cilantro, salt, and pepper to taste.

5. Arrange the mango slices on a plate or in a bowl (be sure to make it look fancy) and top with the ceviche. Serve right away.

scallop ceviche with mango–aji amarillo dressing

Another amazing, colorful ceviche, this one is drizzled with a mango-aji dressing right before you serve it. The key is beautiful fresh scallops that are marked as "dry" (no, not "dried"), which means they weren't packed in preservative-filled water.

SERVES 4 AS AN APPETIZER

½ pound dry scallops

Juice of 2 limes, or more to taste

Juice of 2 red grapefruits (preferably Ruby Red)

1 small red bell pepper, stemmed, seeded, and cut into ¼-inch cubes

¼ English cucumber (about ¼ pound), peeled and diced into ¼-inch cubes

3 tablespoons finely chopped red onion

1 red grapefruit

¼ cup Mango–Aji Amarillo Puree (page 124)

¼ cup mayonnaise

Tortilla chips, for serving

1. Dice the scallops into small cubes, about ¼ inch. Combine them with the lime and grapefruit juices in a large nonmetal bowl, tossing to coat the scallops well with the juice. Cover the surface with plastic wrap and refrigerate, stirring occasionally, until the scallop cubes are white all the way to the center, about 3 hours.

2. Drain off and discard the juice. Combine the scallops with the bell pepper, cucumber, and onion in a clean nonmetal bowl.

3. Slice the rind and pith off the remaining grapefruit. Use a sharp paring knife to slice the grapefruit sections clean away from the membrane, dropping the fruit segments into the bowl with the scallops as you work and turning over the membrane like the pages of a book until all the segments have been trimmed free. Squeeze any remaining juice in the membrane over the scallops.

4. Toss the scallops gently to combine without breaking up the grapefruit. Divide the mixture among four plates. Stir the Mango–Aji Amarillo Puree well with the mayonnaise and drizzle over each plate. Serve with tortilla chips for scooping up the ceviche.

zucchini, jicama, and apple salad

Salad is all about a good mix of textures and a damn tasty dressing. This one has all that: the tender zucchini, the snappy apples, crunchy jicama, and a sweet, tart, and slightly lip-tingling vinaigrette.

SERVES 4 TO 6 AS A SIDE OR APPETIZER

½ cup Mango–Aji Amarillo Puree (page 124)

Juice of 2 limes (3 to 4 tablespoons)

3 tablespoons extra virgin olive oil

2 tablespoons fresh cilantro leaves, chopped

4 tender young zucchini, about 1½ pounds

1 medium jicama

2 Granny Smith apples

Salt

1. In a large bowl, whisk the Mango–Aji Amarillo Puree with the lime juice, olive oil, and cilantro.

2. Cut the ends off the zucchini and slice them, skin on, into 2-inch-long matchsticks. Add them to the dressing.

3. Peel the jicama. Slice it and cut into 2-inch-long matchsticks and add them to the zucchini.

4. Scrub and quarter the apples, discarding the seeds and tough cores, and slice the apple into 2-inch-long matchsticks. Add them to the salad and toss gently. Taste and season with salt, if necessary. Divide among plates or bowls and serve.

chile colorado sauce

In the north of Mexico, where I'm from, chunks of luscious braised pork wade in a ruddy sauce. If the pot was big enough, I swear I'd jump right in.

Just seeing the steaming heap, just smelling the chiles, gives me the kind of happy feeling that a French guy must get when he comes across coq au vin, or a Jewish guy has when he sees a bowl of matzoh ball soup. This is my soul food. This is *carne con chile colorado.*

And no, it's not from the state of Colorado. *Colorado* basically means "red" in Spanish, as in the color imparted by chiles like guajillos and anchos. When I was little and my mom would make this dish, the house would have this unbelievable aroma of tomatoes and tomatillos, garlic and onions, all charring on a *comal.* This more than anything else, my mom always says, is the smell of a Mexican kitchen.

You see this basic combination of ingredients in various forms throughout the country, from that mind-blowing pork to the marinade for thin slices of beef browning over charcoal in the street markets of Oaxaca, to big pots of pozole, the hominy stew that's the world's greatest hangover cure. But my Chile Colorado Sauce distills the flavors into a puree that you can turn into multiple dishes. It's a beautiful thing: a little tangy from the tomatillos, a touch sweet from the tomatoes and onions, and packed with flavor (not heat) from the ancho and guajillo chiles. And making it fills your kitchen with the same awesome smells I was blessed to experience growing up.

chile colorado sauce

MAKES 2 QUARTS

3 medium Spanish or white onions, quartered

8 medium fresh tomatillos, husked and washed

4 plum tomatoes, cored and quartered

8 whole garlic cloves, peeled

Olive oil, for drizzling

1 ancho chile (½ ounce), stemmed, seeded, and deveined

2 guajillo chiles (½ ounce), stemmed, seeded, and deveined

1 quart chicken stock (low-sodium store-bought is fine)

Salt and freshly ground black pepper

1. Preheat the broiler.

2. Put the onions, tomatillos, tomatoes, and garlic on a baking sheet and drizzle them with olive oil. Put the baking sheet under the broiler and cook without turning until the vegetables start to get charred, about 7 minutes. Remove, set aside, and let cool to room temperature.

3. In a large dry skillet over medium-low heat, toast the guajillos, turning them over halfway through, just until they smell great, about 1 minute. Transfer them to a bowl, cover them with hot water, and let them soak until they're soft, about 30 minutes. Drain the chiles and discard the soaking water.

4. Combine the vegetables and chiles in a blender with the chicken stock (you'll have to work in batches) and puree until the mixture is very smooth. Transfer each batch to a bowl as it's done, and stir the batches together well. Season with salt and pepper to taste.

5. Store it in an airtight container in the refrigerator for up to a week or in the freezer for up to a month.

SIMPLE WAYS TO USE IT

- Let pork, chicken, or beef hang out in it for a few hours, throw the meat on the grill, and you're a happy camper.

- Use it instead of the Roasted Tomatillo Salsa to make Chilaquiles (page 85).

- Thin it with some chicken stock and you have a killer base for soup or the liquid for some truly amazing braising—think pork butt, belly, ribs, tongue!

DRIED CHILES

It's hard to overstate the role dried chiles play in Mexican cooking. You know how almost everyone in the United States has one of those little jars of red pepper flakes in his cupboard? Well, compare that to a Mexican household, where giant bags of dried chiles are crammed into the pantry. They're the secret to so many soups and moles, marinades and salsas. And once you learn how easy it is to use them, your kitchen will never be the same.

You know how flavorful fresh chiles can be. Drying only concentrates their essence. For instance, take the mild chile starring in this chapter's mother sauce. No one I know eats the fresh chiles that are dried to make guajillos—probably because they're so freaking good dried. They're bright, earthy, and a little citrusy and contribute a gorgeous brick-red color.

Look for the freshest dried chiles you can get your hands on—just because they're dried doesn't mean they last forever. They should have stems and be soft enough that you can bend them in half without breaking them. When you find good ones, buy a lot and store them in an airtight jar or bag in a cool, dark place. They'll keep for months. The best way to prevent them from drying out is to make a big batch of the Chile Colorado Sauce and freeze it. You know you want to!

TOASTING DRIED CHILES

To unlock the flavor power of ancho and guajillo chiles for any dish you plan to make, all you have to do is toast them and soak them. Here's how:

- Cut a slit in the side of the chiles and dump out the seeds. Scrape the insides with your knife to get out any seeds stuck to the chile.

- Heat a dry skillet over medium-low heat.

- Drop in the chiles (work in batches to avoid crowding the pan) and flip them and press down on them with tongs until they smell awesome. Be careful not to burn them.

- As an alternative, you can spread out the chiles on a baking sheet and toast them in the oven at 400°F. The second you smell their awesomeness, pull them out.

- Now you've released their natural oils.

  Once you've soaked them in hot water for 30 minutes or so, so they get soft and fleshy, you're ready to rock. You can even use the chile-infused water to help puree them with the rest of your ingredients.

ROASTING THE VEGETABLES

Here's why this recipe is so tasty: You have those beautiful toasted chiles and you combine them with beautiful roasted vegetables. With that formula, it's tough to go wrong. Now, some people roast them painstakingly, first the garlic and onions, then the tomatoes and tomatillos, on a *comal*. But I've found that the results are equally awesome if you just toss them in a little oil and roast them all at once in a really hot oven or on your grill. And don't be afraid of getting some char on those babies—that's how Mexicans roll.

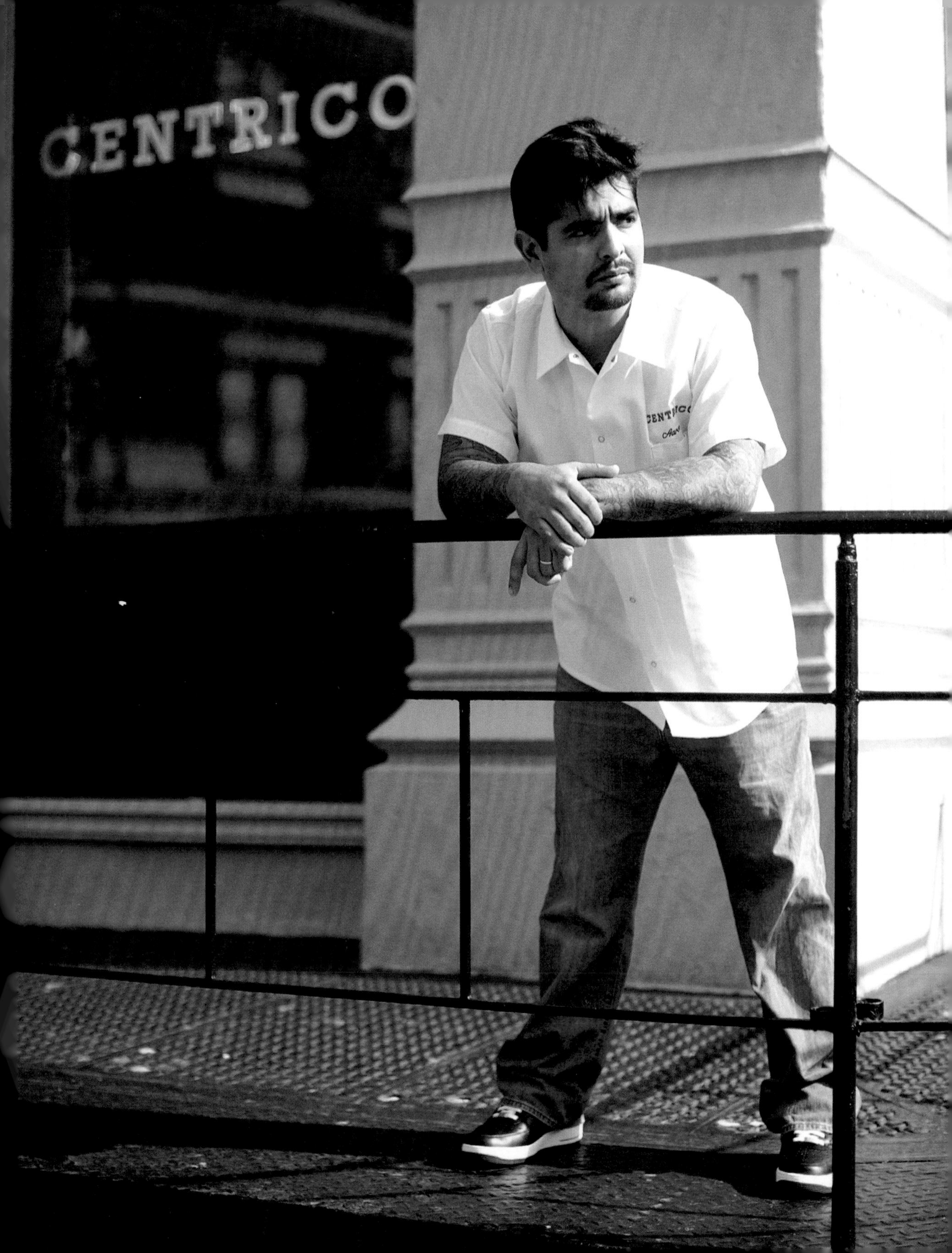
CENTRICO

tacos de chivo *goat (or lamb) tacos*

Watch your friends' eyes light up all around you when you haul this perfect pile of tender, tasty meat to the table. And as they grab warm tortillas, top their own tacos, and sing your praises, try to resist telling them how easy it was to make.

MAKES 16 TO 24 TACOS

One 3½- to 4-pound bone-in cut of goat (*chivo*) or lamb, such as shoulder or leg

Salt

2 cups Chile Colorado Sauce (page 134)

accompaniments

16 to 24 corn tortillas

Sliced radishes

Roasted Tomatillo Salsa (page 78)

Chopped fresh cilantro

Chopped white onion

Lime wedges

1. Put the rack in the middle of the oven and preheat the oven to 350°F.

2. Put the meat in a shallow 3-quart baking dish. Generously season the meat with salt. Pour the Chile Colorado Sauce over the meat and rub it on all sides of the meat. Cover the dish tightly with two layers of foil and cook in the oven until the meat is very tender, 3 to 3½ hours.

3. Take the dish from the oven (keep the oven on), remove and reserve the foil, and let the meat cool in its liquid for about 30 minutes.

4. When it's cool enough to handle, coarsely shred the meat with your fingers or forks, discarding the bones. Return the meat to the cooking liquid, stir, cover the dish again with the foil, and return it the oven until the sauce is hot, about 30 minutes.

5. After about 15 minutes, make two stacks of tortillas, wrap the stacks in foil, and put them in the oven to heat.

6. Serve the meat in the baking dish with the tortillas and other accompaniments in bowls alongside, and let everyone assemble their own tacos at the table.

sautéed shrimp with creamy red chile salsa

Once you have my Chile Colorado Sauce in your fridge or freezer, a seriously delicious dinner is just minutes away. Shrimp sautéed with a little garlic always makes good eating, but add Chile Colorado Sauce and heavy cream (don't worry, *papi*, just a little), and it's off the hook. White rice works beautifully to soak up that sauciness, but try it with grits!

SERVES 4

¼ cup olive oil

4 garlic cloves, thinly sliced

2 pounds jumbo shrimp, peeled and deveined

1 cup Chile Colorado Sauce (page 134)

½ cup heavy cream

1 tablespoon chopped fresh cilantro

Cooked rice, polenta, or grits, for serving

Lime wedges, for serving

1. Combine the olive oil and garlic in a large skillet. Put it over medium heat and cook, stirring frequently, until the garlic turns light brown.

2. Turn the heat to high, add the shrimp (in batches if necessary), and cook them for 1 minute on each side. Return all the shrimp to the skillet, lower the heat to medium, and pour the Chile Colorado Sauce and heavy cream over them. Cook until the shrimp are just cooked through, about 5 minutes.

3. Scoop out the shrimp with a slotted spoon and set them aside. Simmer the sauce until it thickens, 3 to 4 minutes.

4. Add the cilantro and return the shrimp to the sauce. Turn down the heat and reheat the shrimp gently.

5. Spoon the shrimp and sauce into bowls over rice, polenta, or grits, and serve immediately with lime wedges.

pozole rojo

I think my nose is outfitted with pozole GPS. Anytime I'm in Mexico and hunger strikes, I can sniff out a great bowl whether I know the neighborhood or not. Compulsively slurpable, this hearty soup starts out delicious—an aromatic chile-spiked broth floating with hominy—and after you're done topping it with chopped onions, herbs, and crunchy fried tortilla strips, it's table-slapping good.

SERVES 8

One 6-pound boneless pork butt

1 quart chicken stock (low-sodium store-bought is fine)

1 head garlic, separated into cloves and peeled

Salt

1 teaspoon dried whole oregano (preferably Mexican), crumbled

2½ cups Chile Colorado Sauce (page 134)

Three 15-ounce cans white hominy, drained

garnish

Vegetable oil, for frying

8 corn tortillas, cut into thin strips

Finely chopped white onion

Thinly sliced radishes

Lime wedges

Dried whole oregano (preferably Mexican), crumbled

1. Put the pork in a large heavy stockpot or Dutch oven. Add 3 quarts water, the stock, garlic, and 1 teaspoon salt and bring to a boil. Skim off and discard any foam that rises to the surface. Stir in the oregano, reduce the heat, and simmer gently, uncovered, until the pork is tender, about 3 hours.

2. Lift the pork out of the broth onto a cutting board. Shred the pork with two forks and return it to the broth along with the Chile Colorado Sauce and hominy and another teaspoon of salt.

3. Bring to a boil, then reduce the heat and simmer for 30 minutes.

4. While the pozole cooks, line a baking sheet with paper towels. Pour ½ inch of vegetable oil into a large skillet over medium-high heat. When the surface shimmers but the oil is not smoking (if it is, reduce the heat!), fry the tortilla strips in batches—so you don't crowd the skillet—just until they're golden brown, about 3 minutes per batch. Transfer them to the paper towels to drain and sprinkle them very lightly with salt while they're still hot.

5. Serve bowls of pozole with the tortilla strips and bowls of onion, radish slices, lime wedges, and oregano and let your guests garnish their own servings.

roasted turkey with red chile gravy

I get why people save turkey for Thanksgiving. I would, too, if mine was the same old bird. But imagine if your turkey was infused with the flavors of my easy Chile Colorado Sauce—garlic, tangy tomatillo, and magical, citrusy guajillo chiles. And instead of that sludgy brown gravy from a jar, yours was a combo of chicken stock, those tasty brown bits at the bottom of the roasting pan, and another dose of that chile sauce, mild in spice but blowing the roof off with flavor.

SERVES 8 TO 10

1 turkey (approximately 14 pounds), thoroughly thawed if frozen

Salt

1½ cups Chile Colorado Sauce (page 134)

2 tablespoons unsalted butter, softened, plus more if necessary

1 quart chicken stock (low-sodium store-bought is fine)

⅓ cup all-purpose flour

1. The night before you plan to roast the turkey, pat the skin completely dry with paper towels and sprinkle salt lightly all over the skin. Rub about 1 teaspoon salt inside the walls of the turkey cavity. Rub ½ cup of the Chile Colorado Sauce all over the turkey, reaching under the skin to massage it into the breast meat and rubbing a few spoonfuls inside the cavity. Wrap the flap of neck skin down over the cavity, tucking it under the body, and tuck the wing tips up under the breast. Set the turkey on a rack in a roasting pan and cover it loosely with plastic wrap. Let it marinate overnight in the refrigerator.

2. At least 1 hour before you'll cook it, remove the turkey from the refrigerator and let it stand uncovered so it comes to room temperature. Position an oven rack in the lower third of the oven and preheat the oven to 350°F. While the oven is heating, rub the 2 tablespoons butter all over the skin of the turkey. Pour a cup of water into the bottom of the roasting pan.

3. Roast the turkey for 1 hour.

(continued)

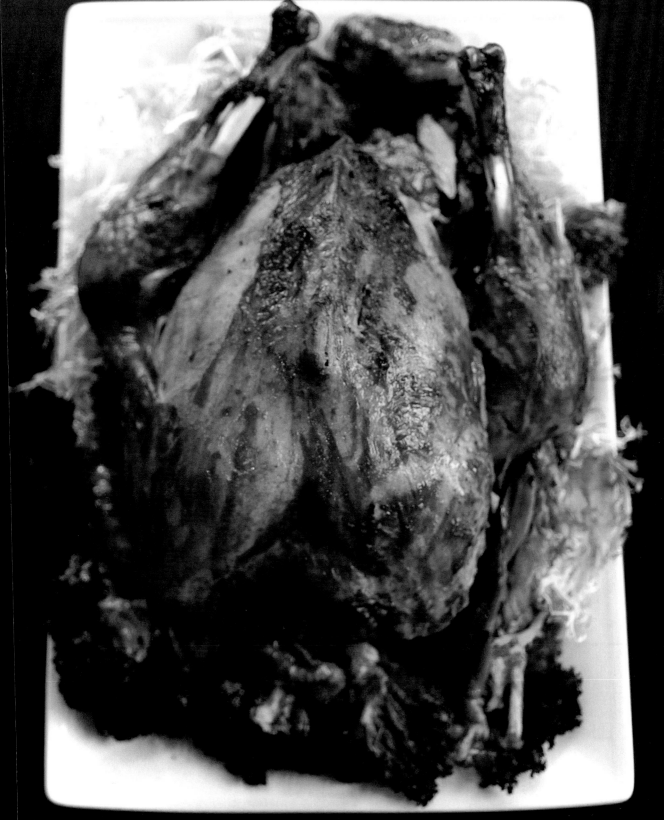

4. Remove the bird from the oven and brush it all over with ½ cup of the Chile Colorado Sauce. Pour another cup of water into the bottom of the pan. Tent the turkey loosely with a sheet of foil and return it to the oven. Roast the turkey until an instant-read thermometer inserted into the thickest part of the thigh reaches 170°F, 2 to 3 hours more. Check it occasionally after 2 hours. If the bottom of the pan gets dry during roasting, add a little more water, ½ cup at a time.

5. Transfer the turkey to a serving platter and let it rest for 30 minutes. (During this time, the temperature in the thigh will rise to 175°F.)

6. Meanwhile, make the gravy. Pour the pan juices into a heatproof glass 2-cup measure. Add ½ cup of the chicken stock to the juices in the roasting pan and swirl it, scraping up any browned bits with a wooden spoon. Pour it all into the measuring cup. Skim off the fat, reserving it in a separate cup. If the pan juices and chicken stock do not make up 2 cups, add more chicken stock to make 2 cups.

7. Put 6 tablespoons of the reserved fat in a large heavy saucepan over medium heat. (If there is not enough fat, add butter until you have 6 tablespoons total.) Whisk in the flour and the remaining ½ cup Chile Colorado Sauce, and cook over medium heat, whisking continually for 3 minutes, until the mixture is very thick. Pour in the pan juices in a thin, steady stream, whisking constantly to avoid lumps. Whisk in the remaining chicken stock and bring the mixture to a boil. Reduce the heat and simmer, whisking now and then, until the gravy is thick and smooth, 12 to 15 minutes. Season with salt to taste.

8. Serve the turkey with the gravy.

birria *mexican stew*

Whenever this deep-red stew is bubbling away on my stove and I'm smelling those chiles and spices, I close my eyes and imagine myself in Mexico at one of the taquerias that specialize in this meltingly tender lamb or beef piled on tortillas and almost always served with a little bowl of the unbelievably tasty cooking liquid alongside. In my version, I add pork to the equation (Why? Why not!) and keep the meat and broth together in delicious matrimony. Serve it with your favorite starch: mashed potatoes, polenta, or even buttered egg noodles.

SERVES 6

2 tablespoons olive oil

1 pound beef top round, cubed for stew

1 pound baby back pork ribs, cut into 1-inch pieces by your butcher

2½ quarts beef or chicken stock (low-sodium store-bought is fine)

1 medium white or yellow onion, coarsely chopped

6 whole garlic cloves, peeled

1 cup Chile Colorado Sauce (page 136)

2 fresh or dried bay leaves

Finely chopped leaves of 6 sprigs fresh thyme

1 tablespoon dried whole oregano (preferably Mexican)

Salt and freshly ground black pepper

2 limes, cut into wedges, for serving

1. Heat a large, deep heavy pot or Dutch oven over medium heat. Pour in the olive oil, and working in batches to avoid crowding your pan, brown the beef and ribs on all sides, transferring the meat to a plate as it's browned.

2. Pour in the stock and stir in the onion and garlic, scraping the browned bits from the pan with a wooden spoon. Return all the meat to the pot, bring to a boil, then reduce the heat and cook at a gentle simmer for 1 hour, until the meats are almost tender.

3. Stir in the Chile Colorado Sauce, bay leaves, thyme, oregano, and salt and pepper to taste. Simmer until the meat is tender, about 30 minutes more. Add more salt if necessary.

4. Serve the stew in big bowls with lime wedges on the side for squeezing.

pickled onions, my way

A love for pickling is contagious. When I worked for Douglas Rodriguez, one of my culinary mentors, I watched as he garnished everything from salads to ceviches with pickled shallots and habaneros. When I hung out with Michael Symon while we competed on *The Next Iron Chef*, I saw a man as committed to pickling as I am to chiles.

Nowadays, finding a chef who doesn't pickle is like discovering a bird without wings—it's almost unnatural. And it's not just a trend. Not only does soaking ingredients in tasty vinegar solution preserve them, it adds a whole new dimension of flavor. It's like a flavor genie snuck inside your vegetable or fruit and injected a ton of brightness and acidity.

While you might not think of Mexico as pickle country, most taquerias and torta shops have a vat of vinegar-soaked jalapeños. And just about any order of the Yucatecan miracle known as *cochinita pibil* (page 120) comes topped with the pinkish pickled onions that inspired this chapter. I mean, what could be better after a big bite of rich, meltingly tender pork than a rush of acidity to refresh your palate and prepare it for that next bite of pork? I apply that same tasty logic to wonderfully starchy ingredients like yucca and plantains (when they're ripe and sweet or green and savory). In fact, it'd be tough to think of a dish that doesn't benefit from a pickle.

pickled onions, my way

MAKES ABOUT 2 CUPS

1½ cups red wine vinegar

2 tablespoons sugar

1 tablespoon kosher salt

6 whole cloves

2 dried bay leaves

1 teaspoon freshly ground
    black pepper

1 teaspoon dried whole oregano
    (preferably Mexican)

1 whole chile de árbol, or ¼ teaspoon
    red pepper flakes

2 large red onions, thinly sliced

1. Combine the vinegar, 1 cup water, the sugar, salt, cloves, bay leaves, black pepper, oregano, and chile de árbol in a heavy medium nonreactive saucepan and set it over medium-high heat. Bring to a boil.

2. Add the onion slices, separating them into individual rings. Let the mixture come back to a boil, then reduce the heat and cook until the onions soften and wilt, 3 to 4 minutes.

3. Remove the saucepan from the heat, cover, and let the mixture cool completely. Transfer the onions and their pickling liquid to a quart-size glass jar or divide among plastic storage containers. Cover and refrigerate for 1 day before serving. Store in an airtight container in the refrigerator for up to 2 weeks.

SIMPLE WAYS TO USE IT

- Brighten up your burgers with a few rings of pickled onions.

- Toss them into hearty salads, like those made with potatoes, roasted beets, or chunks of citrus and avocado.

- Add them to simple ceviches, like shrimp, mango, and avocado spritzed with lots of lime.

PICKLE TIME

I've seen too many people get turned off to pickling by complicated instructions that involve sterilizing jars. That way is awesome if you're down for a kitchen project and want your pickles to last for many months on the shelf. But me? I prefer the quick-and-easy method. Basically, you boil vinegar with spices, soak the onions overnight, and, boom, you've got pickles that'll last you a week or two in the fridge. This is where you can really have fun, integrating other spices that you like or adding a little sugar for sweetness. So get your pickle on!

BEYOND ONIONS

Don't think you're limited to onions, either. I love the way they retain their sweetness and crunch in pickle form, but you should feel free to toss in other stuff alongside the raw onions. Garlic slices! Strips of seeded jalapeños! Cucumber and radish slices!

yucca with onions

Take a look at the ingredients in this recipe, and they'll tell you a little something about yucca, in case you didn't already know: It's so delicious it barely needs anything else! Also called manioc or cassava, depending on what country the folks selling it hail from, this tuber is sort of like a really, really hearty potato. Add a little of my pickled onions, with their tartness and light crunch, and you've got a killer side dish.

SERVES 4

1 pound yucca, peeled and cut into 2-inch chunks

Salt and freshly ground black pepper

½ cup Pickled Onions, My Way (page 150), drained

Fresh cilantro, for garnish

1. Put the yucca in a medium saucepan, cover it with cold water, add a large sprinkle of salt, and bring to a boil. Cook the yucca until very tender, about 30 minutes.

2. Drain the yucca, season generously with salt and pepper, and serve it in a bowl, topped with the Pickled Onions, My Way. Garnish with chopped fresh cilantro.

tacos de carne asada *beef tacos*

Skirt steak is just about the perfect cut—it's got major beefy flavor, it's tender but has a little chew to it, and it's light on the wallet. Tuck charred slices into a warm tortilla with a little salsa, and you're in taco heaven. You could skip the pickled onion marinade and still have an amazing meal, but trust me, it's worth a little extra effort.

MAKES 8 TACOS

One 2-pound skirt steak, trimmed of excess fat

1 cup Pickled Onions, My Way (page 150), drained

Salt and freshly ground black pepper

16 corn tortillas

¼ cup finely chopped white onion

¼ cup chopped fresh cilantro

½ cup Roasted Tomatillo Salsa (page 78) or Roasted Tomato–Chile de Árbol Salsa (page 52)

Radishes, cut into matchsticks, for garnish

Lime wedges, for garnish

1. Put the steak on a platter and cover it with the Pickled Onions, My Way. Turn the steak over and let it sit at room temperature, covered, for 1 hour.

2. Discard the onions. Preheat the grill to high or preheat the broiler.

3. Generously season both sides of the steak with salt and pepper. Put the steak on the grill or under the broiler, and cook for 5 to 6 minutes on each side for medium-rare.

4. Let it rest on a cutting board for 5 minutes, then slice thinly.

5. Warm the corn tortillas for 30 seconds on each side in a dry cast-iron skillet over medium heat. Or wrap the tortillas in foil and heat in a warm oven. Stack 2 tortillas together, place the meat in the center of the tortillas, and top with the chopped onion and cilantro. Drizzle about a teaspoon of Roasted Tomatillo Salsa or Roasted Tomato–Chile de Árbol Salsa on top of each taco. Garnish with radish matchsticks and lime wedges and serve right away.

patacón pisado

Here's a perfect party pass-around that puts a twist on bean dip. Instead of chips, you've got crispy slices of green plantain smeared with a simple, delicious spread made from red beans. A little salty cheese and sweet, tangy pickled onions on top, and you're golden.

SERVES 6 AS AN APPETIZER

¼ pound dried red beans (½ to ¾ cup)

1 dried bay leaf

4 green plantains (about 1½ pounds)

¼ cup olive oil

1 medium white onion, finely chopped

4 garlic cloves, very finely chopped

2 tablespoons ground cumin

¼ cup dried whole oregano (preferably Mexican)

¼ cup tomato paste

Salt and freshly ground black pepper

Corn oil, for frying

1 cup Pickled Onions, My Way (page 150), drained

1 cup grated cotija (preferably the Cacique brand)

1. Put the beans in a medium saucepan with the bay leaf and add enough water to cover the beans. Bring to a simmer and cook until the beans are tender and no longer mealy, 1 to 2 hours. Drain the beans and set them aside. Discard the bay leaf.

2. Half-fill a large saucepan with cold water and bring it to a boil. Trim each end off the plantains and make two long cuts, just through the skin, along the sides of each. Boil the plantains whole for 20 seconds, then remove and run under cold water. Remove and discard the skin. Cut the plantains crosswise in ½-inch-thick slices. Set aside.

3. Put the olive oil, chopped onion, and garlic in a medium skillet and set it over medium heat. Cook until the onion and garlic are tender and slightly browned, 5 minutes. Add the cumin and oregano and cook, stirring occasionally, for another 2 minutes. Stir in the tomato paste and cooked beans. Transfer to a food processor and process to a fairly smooth paste. Season with salt and pepper to taste.

4. Heat ¼ inch of corn oil in a large cast-iron skillet over medium heat until the oil registers 300°F on a deep-fry thermometer. Fry the plantain slices in batches until they're tender and golden brown.

5. Transfer the plantain slices to a paper towel–lined plate. Once you have fried all of them, use a spatula to lay each piece on a cutting board and use the flat side of the spatula to press each slice flat, to a thickness of about ¼ inch. Working in batches, refry the slices briefly, 1 to 2 minutes, until golden brown all over. Transfer them to fresh paper towels to drain.

6. Spread a layer of the bean puree over the fried plantains, add some of the Pickled Onions, My Way, and sprinkle each one with some of the cheese. Serve right away.

tostones with olives
and pickled onions

You might not come across this version of *tostones*, flattened, fried green plantains, at your local Cuban or Dominican restaurant, but one taste and you'll wish they'd put it on the menu. The addition of olives delivers an irresistible saltiness that goes so well with the starchy plantain and tangy pickled onions. Another perfect pass-around appetizer.

SERVES 4 TO 6 AS AN APPETIZER

6 medium black olives (preferably oil-cured)

½ cup crumbled queso fresco (preferably the Cacique brand) or lightly salty feta

1 tablespoon crema fresca (preferably the Cacique brand) or sour cream

2 teaspoons extra virgin olive oil

1 teaspoon crumbled chile pequin or cayenne pepper

1 tablespoon chopped fresh cilantro

1 teaspoon chopped fresh chives

Fine salt and freshly ground black pepper

2 large green plantains

Vegetable oil, for frying

2 tablespoons coarsely chopped Pickled Onions, My Way (page 150)

1. Remove the pits, if any, from the olives and finely chop the olives. Stir the olives together in a small bowl with the queso fresco, crema fresca, olive oil, chile, cilantro, and chives. Try some, and season with salt if you'd like, and a couple of grindings of pepper. Cover and refrigerate until you need it.

2. Half-fill a large saucepan with cold water and bring it to a boil. Trim each end off the plantains and make two long cuts, just through the skin, along the sides of each. Boil the plantains whole for 20 seconds, then remove and run under cold water. Remove and discard the skin. Cut the plantains crosswise in ½-inch-thick slices.

3. Pour ¼ inch of vegetable oil into a large cast-iron skillet and heat it over medium-high heat until the oil shimmers. Working in batches, add the plantain slices in a single layer. Fry them, turning them over once, until they're lightly golden on both sides, about 2 minutes per side. Sprinkle with fine salt.

4. To serve, smear a little of the black olive mixture on top of each *tostone* and top each with a few shreds of the Pickled Onions, My Way. Serve the *tostones* right away, while they are still warm.

mole, my way

I wasn't your average kid. While some little boys were watching cartoons, I was peering into pots of my mom's bubbling moles. She ran a catering business out of our apartment, which often overwhelmed the small kitchen. I remember my first time helping her make a huge batch of mole one day. I was toasting a ton of *chiles pasillas* on a few hot *comals* (the large flat pans that are a staple in Mexican kitchens). Next thing I knew, my mom and I were coughing and choking, jetting out of our apartment, away from the smoke. Soon our neighbors came spilling out, too. I had burned the pasillas, and the whole building had to be evacuated. The lesson I learned that day is one I'd never forget: Respect the chile.

After the fire trucks left, the cooking resumed. Tomatillos and tomatoes were roasted. Onions and garlic, too. There were fruit and nuts frying, the blender whirring, and before I knew it, a dark liquid was simmering in a giant pot. When it was ready, my mom dipped in a spoon and let me taste it. Forget world peace—this was the ultimate example of harmony. All the ingredients came together to make one thing I'd never forget.

Mole is not a sauce—it's a whole category of them. From the Nahuatl word *molli*, meaning "to grind," moles used to be (and in some places, still are) made by grinding each ingredient on a metate, a sort of flat, pre-Hispanic mortar and pestle. And since moles often have a lot of ingredients, you can be grateful to live in the Age of the Blender. Some people assume you just add everything to a pot and there's mole. Nope, not happening. It's about treating everything separately—toasting the chiles, roasting the tomatillos and tomatoes, maybe frying the nuts. Then you puree it all, and cook that puree in a little fat, which brings it all together.

In the state of Oaxaca alone, you'll find at least seven different moles, from a soupy, herbaceous green one to another that's thick and jet-black. Every state has its own distinct mole. Really, almost any sauce that has been thickened with seeds, bread, tortillas, or masa can be considered a mole. But none have reached as far as *mole poblano*. This dark brown sauce famously laced with a little chocolate comes from the state of Puebla, and it's what most people think of when they hear the word "mole." It's also one of my favorites. This is my homage to it.

Like all moles, the exact formula is up to the cook. I use my chile trifecta—a combination of smoky anchos, sweet raisiny pasillas, and citrusy guajillos—to achieve an amazingly complex flavor and rich color. There's a little dried fruit and chocolate in there, just enough to give the sauce some sweetness and depth. But remember, this isn't Hershey's syrup, it's mole. Then there's my touch— red wine—that only sounds weird until you dip in your spoon and have your first taste.

SIMPLE WAYS TO USE IT

- Got leftover roast chicken, Thanksgiving turkey, lamb, or duck? Just about any meat warmed in this mole tastes like dinner in Puebla. If you're starting with uncooked meat, brown it in a pan, then add it to the simmering mole.

- Have fun with it: Mix ¼ cup with 8 tablespoons (1 stick) softened butter for a mole compound butter! Next time you roast a chicken, tuck that underneath the skin.

- Add a little to your chocolate, pumpkin, or carrot cake batter. That may sound batty, until you remember all the dessert-friendly stuff in the mole—dried fruit, Mexican cinnamon, and chocolate!

PLAN OF ATTACK

This mole is by far the most complicated recipe in this book. Before you get overwhelmed, know that I got you. First of all, you don't make a cup of mole. Because it's a little labor intensive, I have you make a big batch. It freezes so well, why wouldn't you? That means a couple hours of work equals many, many great meals. You can store mole in an airtight container in the refrigerator for two weeks.

The other secret to making moles low stress is getting organized and having a strategy. So if you are not up to making the whole recipe in one day, here's an alternate game plan, my gift to you:

The Night Before
Toast and grind the spices. Store the chiles and ground spices in separate airtight bags in a cool place.

The Morning Of
Seed, toast, and soak the chiles. Once they're soft, store them in the soaking water in the fridge. Roast the vegetables. Once they're cooled, cover them and pop them in the fridge until you're ready to cook the mole.

DRIED CHILES

Remember to look for chiles that have stems and are soft enough that you can bend them in half without their cracking or snapping. Using old, brittle chiles in your mole is like drinking wine a week after it was opened—it won't kill you, but it sure as hell won't taste very good. For more on seeding and toasting dried chiles, go to pages 135 and 136.

SWEET PLANTAINS

Plantains are basically big starchy bananas that Latinos love dearly. We eat them in all stages of ripeness, but for this recipe, you want them really ripe. Now, here's where people sometimes go wrong. When a regular banana is ripe, the skin turns yellow. When it starts turning black, most people toss it in the trash. Forget that. I want you to use plantains whose skins are almost totally black. That means they're very sweet and soft, and will add the right flavor and texture to the mole. Look for them at this stage at the store or buy them yellow and keep them in a warm spot until they turn black, about two weeks.

mole, my way *aka mole sánchez*

MAKES 1 GALLON

½ pound guajillo chiles (about 32), stemmed, seeded, and deveined

½ pound pasilla chiles (about 24), stemmed, seeded, and deveined

½ pound ancho chiles (about 16), stemmed, seeded, and deveined

2 medium yellow onions, quartered

4 medium tomatoes, cored and quartered

10 fresh tomatillos (about 1 pound), husked and rinsed

8 large whole garlic cloves, peeled

1 cup pitted prunes

1 cup dried apricots

½ cup raisins

1 bottle red wine

2 tablespoons dried whole oregano (preferably Mexican)

1 tablespoon cumin seeds

1 tablespoon fennel seeds

2 tablespoons black peppercorns

5 whole cloves

2 large canela (Mexican cinnamon) or 4 cinnamon sticks

4 quarts chicken stock (low-sodium store-bought is fine)

2 sweet (black) plantains (about ¾ pound)

Vegetable oil

1 ounce Mexican chocolate

5 corn tortillas, charred over an open flame until blackened in spots

Salt

1. Preheat the oven to 500°F.

2. Spread the guajillo, pasilla, and ancho chiles on a baking sheet and put in the oven. Cook for 2 minutes, or until they're fragrant. Take the pan out of the oven (leave the oven on), transfer the chiles to a large bowl or pot, and pour in enough water to cover them. Let the chiles soak until they're soft, about 45 minutes.

3. Meanwhile, put the onions, tomatoes, tomatillos, and garlic on a clean baking sheet and roast in the oven until the vegetables are slightly charred, about 7 minutes. Take the pan out of the oven and set it aside.

4. Combine the prunes, apricots, and raisins with the red wine in a medium saucepan. Bring it to a strong simmer and cook until the fruit has absorbed most of the wine and the remaining liquid is syrupy, about 10 minutes. Set aside.

5. Heat a dry medium skillet over medium-low heat. Sprinkle in the oregano, cumin seeds, fennel seeds, peppercorns, cloves, and canela. Cook, stirring constantly so as not to burn the spices, until they just begin to smoke. The moment they do, transfer them to a spice grinder and grind to a fine powder.

6. Drain the chiles and discard the soaking water. Combine the chiles, vegetables, fruits, and ground spices in a very large heavy-bottomed pot. Pour in the chicken stock, bring to a simmer, and cook, stirring occasionally, for about 30 minutes, until the flavors meld.

7. Meanwhile, peel the plantains (just as you peel bananas) and slice them crosswise into 1-inch-thick pieces. Heat 3 inches of oil in a deep skillet over medium heat and fry the plantain slices (in batches, if necessary) until they're golden. Scoop them out with a slotted spoon or skimmer and add them to the mole pot along with the chocolate and tortillas. Simmer for 15 minutes more.

8. Remove the pot from the heat and let the mixture cool to room temperature. Puree the mole in batches in a blender until it's very smooth. Season with salt to taste. Store in airtight containers in the refrigerator for up to 2 weeks or freeze for up to 3 months.

roasted cornish game hens with mole

Whenever I hit up a great Chinese restaurant and order Peking duck, I'm struck by how much the whole experience reminds me of eating tacos. There you are, with awesome meat, a great sauce, and little pancakes or buns to pile it all on. Okay, maybe that's just a Mexican guy talking. Still, give this a shot—the meat from perfectly roasted, crisp-skinned Cornish game hens on tortillas with my mole, which you have to admit looks a bit like hoisin sauce.

SERVES 4

2 Cornish game hens (about 1¾ pounds each)

Olive oil

4 garlic cloves, very finely chopped

Salt and freshly ground black pepper

2 cups Mole, My Way (page 166)

Warm corn tortillas, for serving

6 scallions, thinly sliced

1. Preheat the oven to 375°F.

2. Pat the hens dry with a paper towel and rub all over with olive oil. Rub the garlic over the outside and massage it under the skin on the breast. Rub with more olive oil, and sprinkle generously with salt and pepper.

3. Put the hens on a rack over a rimmed baking sheet. Roast them until an instant-read thermometer inserted into the thickest part of the thigh reads 165°F, 35 to 40 minutes.

4. Transfer the hens to a platter and let them rest for 10 minutes while you warm the Mole, My Way, in a small saucepan.

5. Carve the birds and pull the meat off the bones, leaving the skin on. Serve the meat on a platter along with warm tortillas and the heated mole. To eat, lay some meat on a tortilla, spoon on a generous amount of mole, and sprinkle with scallions.

turkey enchiladas with mole, my way

Believe it or not, turkey is a traditional mole meat, especially common with *mole poblano*. You'll often find it gently cooked and covered in the sauce. Here, it's tucked into enchiladas, those unbelievably delicious sauce-doused tortillas that you probably thought you'd never be able to make at home.

SERVES 4

3 cups shredded roast turkey

2 cups Mole, My Way (page 166)

About 1 cup vegetable oil

12 corn tortillas

1 cup chicken stock (low-sodium store-bought is fine)

Salt

1 cup shredded queso fresco (preferably the Cacique brand) or lightly salty feta

½ cup crema fresca (preferably the Cacique brand) or crème fraîche

3 tablespoons chopped white onion

3 breakfast radishes, thinly sliced

1. Preheat the oven to 350°F. Line a baking sheet with paper towels.

2. In a medium bowl, toss the turkey with ½ cup of the Mole, My Way. Set aside.

3. Heat ½ inch of oil in a large cast-iron skillet over medium-high heat. When the oil just starts to shimmer, fry the tortillas in batches, about 15 seconds per side. You're just softening them—you're not looking for crunchy tortillas. Drain the tortillas on the paper towels.

4. Pour off all the oil and pour the remaining mole into the skillet. Turn the heat to medium and whisk in the chicken stock until the mixture is smooth. Cook until the mixture is just heated through. Don't let it boil. Taste and season with salt.

5. Dunk a tortilla completely into the sauce, then lay it flat on a plate. Put ¼ cup of the turkey in the center of the tortilla and top with a sprinkle of queso fresco. Fold the tortilla in half and lay it in a 13 by 9-inch baking dish. Repeat with the remaining tortillas, slightly overlapping them as you line them up in the dish. Pour the remaining sauce over the enchiladas. Bake until they're warmed through and the sauce is just bubbling, 10 to 15 minutes.

6. Drizzle with the crema fresca and scatter with the chopped onion and sliced radishes. Serve right away.

braised beef short ribs with mole

The classic way to serve mole is to spoon the rich sauce over simply prepared chicken. But imagine what happens when something as tasty as mole teams up with the ultimate crowd pleaser: absurdly tender beef short ribs, the kind that you can dig into with spoons.

SERVES 8

4 slices bacon, chopped

4 pounds bone-in short ribs, trimmed of excess fat

Salt and freshly ground black pepper

1 large white onion, chopped

4 large garlic cloves, chopped

5 cups beef stock (low-sodium store-bought is fine)

1 cup Mole, My Way (page 166)

2 teaspoons apple cider vinegar

1½ teaspoons whole dried oregano (preferably Mexican), crumbled

1 tablespoon chopped fresh cilantro, for garnish

Sesame seeds and radish matchsticks, for garnish

1. Preheat the oven to 350°F.

2. Heat a large ovenproof pot or Dutch oven over medium-high heat. Cook the bacon until it's brown and crisp. Use a slotted spoon to transfer the bacon to a large bowl.

3. Season the beef with salt and pepper. Working in batches, brown the short ribs on all sides in the bacon fat in the pot, about 5 minutes per batch. Transfer the short ribs to the bowl with the bacon and discard most of the fat in the pot.

4. Add the onion and garlic to the remaining fat in the pot and cook, stirring occasionally, until the onion begins to brown, about 5 minutes. Add ½ cup of the stock. Bring it to a boil, scraping up browned bits in the pot with a wooden spoon. Add back the beef, bacon, and any accumulated juices. Stir in the Mole, My Way; the rest of the stock; the vinegar; oregano; and 2 teaspoons salt. Bring to a boil, cover the pot, and put it in the oven. Cook until the meat is falling off the bone, about 2½ hours.

5. Serve it from the pot at the table, garnished with the cilantro, sesame seeds, and radish, spooning it into bowls for your guests.

dulce de leche

This is the stuff you dream of. The stuff you've licked off your plate when you thought no one was looking.

Think of it as Latin America's Nutella. It's that go-to sweet thing that you could put on just about anything and make it taste awesome. Pale brown, creamy, and gooey, dulce de leche is essentially caramel made from milk instead of straight sugar. There's nothing quite like it, not even Nutella. Plus, when was the last time you could tell your guests that you made Nutella at home?

Of course, you can buy perfectly delicious dulce de leche in a jar or can and use it to make all the recipes in this chapter. But come on, you know you can't beat molten caramel, still warm from the stove. Plus, my method is incredibly easy. So easy that there's really no reason to buy the stuff.

Then comes the fun part. Thinking of all the ways to use it—well, not all of it, because if you're anything like me, by the time you've come up with an idea, you've already crammed a good quarter of your dulce de leche into your mouth.

dulce de leche

MAKES ABOUT 3 CUPS

**Two 14-ounce cans sweetened
condensed milk**

Pour the milk into the top of a double boiler
and put it over a pot of barely simmering
water. Keep the water gently simmering for
2 hours, adding more hot water as the water
evaporates. You don't have to start stirring
until the milk begins to thicken, but once it
does, after about 30 minutes, stir every 15
minutes or so. After 2 hours (if you want it
even darker and funkier, keep cooking for
another hour!), the milk will be all oozy and
golden brown. That, *mis amigos*, is dulce de
leche. Store in an airtight container in the
refrigerator for up to a month.

SIMPLE WAYS TO USE IT

- Toast, butter, dulce de leche. Done.

- Forget fudge: Drizzle this over ice cream for an unforgettable topping.

- Looking to make over your Sunday-morning treat? Swap dulce de leche for maple syrup on pancakes or French toast.

- And speaking of morning, who says you can't stir dulce de leche into your latte? A little while back, I teamed up with Starbucks to make the case that you can—no, *should*.

- Need an easy party dessert? Serve cut-up bananas, pears, and apples along with a dish of dulce de leche for dipping. Or sauté those pieces in butter until they're soft and sweet, then hit them with a dollop of milk caramel.

WHAT'S IN A NAME?

Dulce de leche means, essentially, "milk's sweetness," but that's not the only term Latin Americans use to refer to this magnificently simple sweet treat. Some people call it *manjar,* or basically "food," which should tell you how important the stuff is to its fans. In Colombia, the stuff's called *arequipe,* and in Mexico, we call it *cajeta.* Back in the day people made it with goat's milk.

bananas faustos

This is my take on the classic New Orleans treat, bananas Foster, which ups the ante on an already awesome dessert with the sophisticated flavor of dulce de leche. Excellent on its own, I love to serve it spooned over scoops of vanilla ice cream. The combination of warm sauciness and cold creaminess makes my knees weak.

SERVES 4

2 tablespoons unsalted butter

3 to 4 tablespoons Dulce de Leche (page 174)

3 bananas, peeled and halved lengthwise, then crosswise

¼ cup spiced rum

Vanilla ice cream (optional)

Fresh mint leaves and confectioners' sugar (optional), for garnish

Melt the butter in a medium nonstick skillet over medium heat. Add the Dulce de Leche and mix with a heatproof rubber spatula until they're well combined. Cook for 3 minutes, stirring often. Add the banana slices, stir to coat them, and cook for 3 minutes more. Take the pan off the heat, stir in the rum, and return the pan to the heat. Cook for 2 minutes more, stirring well to coat the bananas with the sauce. Transfer the bananas and sauce to plates, or spoon them over vanilla ice cream. Garnish with fresh mint leaves and confectioners' sugar, if desired.

dulce de leche swirl ice cream

Break out the spoons and invite some friends over. Otherwise, you *will* take down this entire quart of buttery bliss by yourself. I keep the sticky sweetness of the dulce de leche in check with a pinch of salt (trust me, try it!) and an awesomely aromatic vanilla extract from Veracruz. I can't stop thinking about how good a scoop of this looks perched on top of a warm slice of apple pie. For dulce de leche superfans, try it with Bananas Faustos (page 177).

MAKES 1 QUART

2 cups whole milk

1 cup heavy cream

1½ cups Dulce de Leche (page 174)

1 teaspoon pure vanilla extract (preferably from Veracruz)

Salt

1. Heat the milk and cream together in a large heavy saucepan until the mixture just starts to boil. Take the pan off the heat and mix in 1 cup of the Dulce de Leche, stirring until it dissolves. Add the vanilla and a pinch of salt, transfer the mixture to a large bowl, and put the bowl in the refrigerator until it's completely cold. This will take several hours. You can also chill it overnight.

2. Freeze the mixture in an ice cream maker according to the manufacturer's instructions.

3. Spoon about one-quarter of the ice cream into a quart-size freezer container, then dollop on a few spoonfuls of the remaining Dulce de Leche. Continue to layer the ice cream and Dulce de Leche until they're all used up. Freeze the ice cream until it's firm, at least 1 hour, before serving. For storage, press a piece of plastic wrap against the surface of the ice cream before returning it to the freezer.

chile-glazed duck breasts with dulce de leche

Martha Stewart knows good food, so let me brag for a minute about how she raved about these duck breasts when I made them on her show a couple of years back. You will, too, once you dig into those tender pink slices glazed with caramely dulce de leche and smoky spice from ancho chiles.

SERVES 6

3 dried ancho chiles (1¼ ounces), stemmed, seeded, and deveined

1 garlic clove, very finely chopped

½ cup freshly squeezed orange juice

¼ cup Dulce de Leche (page 174)

½ cup chicken stock (low-sodium store-bought is fine)

6 duck breast halves (about ¾ pound each), rinsed, patted dry, and trimmed of excess fat

Salt and freshly ground black pepper

1 tablespoon unsalted butter, cubed

1 tablespoon chopped fresh cilantro

1. Bring 2 cups water to a boil. Heat a dry skillet over medium heat and add the chiles. Toast them, turning them over once, until they've darkened slightly and smell great, about 40 seconds total. Transfer them to a small heatproof bowl and pour the boiling water over them. Set them aside until they're softened, about 20 minutes.

2. Use a slotted spoon to transfer the chiles to a blender. Add 1 cup of the soaking liquid and the garlic and blend until the mixture is smooth. Set it aside.

3. Heat the orange juice in a small saucepan over medium heat, letting it simmer until it has reduced by half. Add the Dulce de Leche and chicken stock, bring the mixture back to a simmer, stirring occasionally, and immediately remove it from the heat and set it aside.

4. Score the skin of the duck (don't cut the flesh) in a diamond pattern with a sharp paring knife. Season the duck generously with salt and pepper. Heat a large heavy-bottomed skillet over medium heat. Working in batches, put in the duck pieces, skin side down, and cook until the skin is well browned.

5. As the fat from the skin renders into the pan, scoop it out with a spoon into a heatproof container and save it for another purpose. Flip the duck over and cook until the meat is browned, about 3 minutes more.

(continued)

Transfer the duck to a plate as it finishes, and repeat the process with the remaining duck breasts.

6. Transfer the duck to a baking tray, cover, and cook until an instant-read thermometer inserted horizontally into the center of a breast registers 135°F (for medium-rare), about 6 minutes. Transfer the duck to a cutting board and let stand, uncovered.

7. Pour out all but 2 tablespoons of the fat from the skillet. Pour the chile puree and reduced juice into the skillet, along with any duck juices that have accumulated on the cutting board. Turn the heat to medium-high and cook, stirring often and scraping up any browned bits on the bottom of the skillet with a wooden spoon, until the mixture has thickened, about 6 minutes. Whisk in the butter until it has melted. Season with salt to taste. Stir in the cilantro.

8. Slice the duck breasts crosswise on a diagonal. Divide the slices among six plates, spoon on the sauce, and serve immediately.

NOTE: Feel free to use chipotles or pasillas instead of anchos, if that's all you can get your mitts on.

ACKNOWLEDGMENTS

To my wife, Ife: Your persistent love and belief in me and all that I do is humbling. You are my partner in life, and all the benefits I've received occurred the moment you entered my world. You are my life.

To my son, Yuma: My heart, and the start of my new life as a father. I want this book to be a constant reminder to you that all your dreams are within reach. I will love you 'til the sun no longer rises.

To my mother, Zarela: You are my foundation, my rock. You're always there to push me and watch proudly over all I do. You drove me to develop my own cooking style and taught me so much about food and how to be a successful chef.

To my stepdaughter, Sofia: Your acceptance of me has warmed my soul. It makes me smile no end to see what a beautiful person you are. The sky is the limit for you.

To my siblings, Marissa, Rodrigo, and Spanky: You've been there through it all, and our friendship and love mean the world to me.

To my business manager and best friend, Andrew Chason: You always have my back, and you'd better believe I'll always have yours. You rock, and I couldn't have done any of this without you.

To my partner, Drew Nieporent: I have learned so much from you about our business. Your standards and expectations for our restaurant, Centrico, have been a source of inspiration for me. Love you, hose man.

To my Taco and better half, Dario Wolos: I can't believe that all the beach conversations and taco excursions have resulted in your dream coming true. I'm happy to know you and to be a part of your future.

To Chef Angel Tenesca: My right hand and a hardworking, badass dude. I appreciate everything you do.

To Tony Penn and the Trifecta crew: Tony, you are my best friend, my annoying uncle, and my mentor all wrapped up into one cool Cali dude.

To Myriad Restaurant Group: The best restaurant outfit in the country—period. Your dedication to your craft is simply awesome.

To my cowriter, JJ Goode: A pro and an unmatched talent. This book is a true testament to your knowledge of and love for food. A rising star without limits. Thank you, thank you, thank you.

To my photographer, Michael Harlan Turkell: I am wowed by how you illuminated my vision for food and made it dance on the pages of this book. I appreciate your patience and flexibility through this whole process.

To my editor, Sarah Branham, and the Atria team: Thank you so much for believing in me and making this book a reality. It's something I'm so proud of. We could not have done it without you.

To Jen Unter: My literary guru and dear friend. Thanks for helping me put this together and helping me share the cuisine I love with the world. You're a rock star.

To Tommy Fijacko: Thanks for assuming the responsibility that is my crazy life and making me look good by being organized and buttoned up.

To Eric Vargas: Your dedication is awesome to see. You will be a great chef one day.

To Allison Page, Brain Lando, Bruce Seidal, Bob Tuschman, Kim Williamson, Brooke Johnson, and all my FoodTV peeps: Thank you so much for giving me the platform to share my love and passion for food with such a large audience. It's been ten-plus years together, and I'm so grateful to you all. THANKS *y mil gracias*!

To the talented and wise chefs who have influenced and supported me throughout the years: Paul Prudhomme, Jonathan Waxman, Douglas Rodriguez, Bobby Flay, Chris Cosentino, John Besh, Marcus Samuelsson, Michael Symon, and, of course, Zarela Martinez.

RESOURCES

Mex Grocer

mexgrocer.com

An excellent source for dried ingredients, canned products, and other cupboard staples. Think chipotles in adobo, pickled jalapeños, hominy, masa harina (corn tortilla flour), huitlacoche, achiote paste, tamarind pulp, and Mexican chocolate.

Kalustyan's

kalustyans.com

For top-notch spices and hard-to-find ingredients, this is the spot. It's where you'll find my beloved aji amarillo paste, Mexican cinnamon and oregano, dried epazote, and ancho chile powder.

Melissa Guerra

melissaguerra.com

If you don't have a good Mexican grocer nearby, don't sweat it—your chile supply is right here. They'll ship you just about any dried Mexican chile imaginable, from anchos and pasillas to árbols and guajillos, as well as Mexican cinnamon and beautiful *molcajetes* (the Mexican mortar and pestle).

The Chile Guy

thechileguy.com

This site is for the truly committed cook. The Chile Guy sells top-notch dried chiles in bulk, for when you're ready to commit to a pound of guajillos or chipotles, and powders and flakes of the highest quality, taste, and consistency.

The Chef's Garden

chefs-garden.com

Farmer Lee Jones and his family farm produce exceptional specialty and heirloom vegetables, herbs, microgreens, and edible flowers that top chefs and restaurants throughout the world recognize as the finest quality available. Their dedication to developing products in new sizes, colors, textures, and flavors is unmatched.

Melissa's

melissas.com

At Melissa's online produce aisle from heaven, you can find all the fresh chiles (serranos, habaneros, poblanos) you need, plus dried chiles and an amazing selection of the funky stuff I love: plantains, passion fruits, and tomatillos.

D'Artagnan

dartagnan.com

For fantastic meat, I've got you covered. This legendary purveyor has everything from great beef, lamb, and pork to tougher-to-find duck breasts, confit legs, and poussins. Cured meats like Spanish chorizo, too.

Cacique

caciqueusa.com

My top pick for delicious Mexican dairy products, such as queso fresco, queso blanco, cotija, and crema fresca. You'll see the Cacique brand in many supermarkets around the country, and if you don't spot it, the website will help you find it.

Las Palmas

laspalmassauce.com

To add an authentic touch to your cooking, look for flavorful Las Palmas brand chile sauces in supermarkets around the country. If you don't spot them, the website will help you find a nearby source.

MOZO Shoes

mozoshoes.com

MOZO® makes revolutionary footwear for creative, passionate, and talented culinary professionals and home cooks who spend a lot of time on their feet. Together we created the first-ever line of signature chef shoes. You can find MOZO shoes at Zappos.com and on the MOZO website.

INDEX

AARÓN SÁNCHEZ is the Food Network star of *Chefs vs. City, Heat Seekers, The Best Thing I Ever Ate, Chopped,* and *Chopped All-Stars*. He is the owner and executive chef of Centrico, located in Manhattan, as well as the culinary face behind Tacombi. He is the son of celebrated Mexican cooking authority Zarela Martinez, and his passion, commitment, and skills have placed him among the country's leading contemporary Latin chefs. He lives in Brooklyn with his wife, singer/songwriter Ife Sánchez Mora, and their two children. Visit www.chefaaronsanchez.com.

JJ GOODE has written about food for *The New York Times, Men's Vogue, Gourmet, Saveur, Bon Appétit, Food & Wine, Every Day with Rachael Ray, ReadyMade, Time Out New York, The Village Voice,* and *Lexus* magazine. He is a contributing editor for *Details,* a former editor at Epicurious.com, and coauthor, with Masaharu Morimoto, of *Morimoto: The New Art of Japanese Cooking,* which was nominated for a James Beard Award and won two IACP Cookbook Awards. He is also the coauthor of *Serious Barbecue,* with Adam Perry Lang. He and his wife live in Brooklyn. Visit www.jjgoode.com.

MICHAEL HARLAN TURKELL, once an aspiring chef, is now a freelance photographer and a photo editor for *Edible Brooklyn* and *Edible Manhattan* magazines. His work was selected for the book *25 Under 25: Up-and-Coming American Photographers V2,* and he has received a Photo District News Photo Annual Award. He also hosts a show on HeritageRadioNetwork.com, *The Food Seen,* which brings together guests working at the intersections of food and art. He is the photographer for *The New Brooklyn Cookbook* and *Clinton Street Baking Co. Cookbook.* Turkell lives in Brooklyn with a cat that had a beer named after it (Masons Black Wheat by Sixpoint Craft Ales). Visit www.harlanturk.com.